Religious Politics
in
Global
and
Comparative Perspective

Recent Titles in Contributions in Sociology

Religious Politics
in
Global
and
Comparative Perspective

Edited by William H. Swatos, Jr.

CONTRIBUTIONS IN SOCIOLOGY, NUMBER 81

GREENWOOD PRESS
New York • Westport, Connecticut • London

Library of Congress Cataloging-in-Publication Data

Religious politics in global and comparative perspective / edited by
    William H. Swatos, Jr.
        p.   cm.—(Contributions in sociology, ISSN 0084–9278 ; no.
81)
    Bibliography: p.
    Includes index.
    ISBN 0–313–26392–2 (lib. bdg. : alk. paper)
    1. Religion and politics.   2. Religion and sociology.   I. Swatos,
William H.   II. Series.
BL65.P7R46   1989
306.6'09'048—dc20   89–2165

British Library Cataloguing in Publication Data is available.

Library of Congress Catalog Card Number: 89–2165
ISBN: 0–313–26392–2
ISSN: 0084–9278

First published in 1989

Greenwood Press, Inc.
88 Post Road West, Westport, Connecticut 06881

Printed in the United States of America

The paper used in this book complies with the
Permanent Paper Standard issued by the National
Information Standards Organization (Z39.48–1984).

10 9 8 7 6 5 4 3 2 1

For
Ed and Anne

Contents

Tables and Figures

TABLES

FIGURES

Acknowledgments

As I indicate in the first chapter, this book is the product of a year's free time released from academic duties as a result of a grant from the World Society Foundation based in the Department of Sociology at the University of Zürich. I am grateful to the foundation—especially its director, Volker Bornschier—for this opportunity. Nothing in the book,however, should be taken as representing the viewpoint of the foundation or any members of its board, though it is certainly my hope that these essays will be found valuable to them as well as to a larger public.

I am also grateful for the assistance of colleagues and associates, especially Colin Campbell, Ron Glassman, and Peter Kivisto. Northern Illinois University was kind enough to administer my grant without fees. The faculties of social science and theology at the University of Iceland, especially in the persons of Björn Björnsson and Pétur Pétursson, gave me opportunity to take my very first stab at presenting the findings that now appear as Chapter 5, and specifically provided the context for the development of the ideas that constitute the final chapter. I particularly benefited from the good fellowship and intellectual stimulation of the Consultation on Implicit Religion at Denton Hall, Yorkshire, and I appreciate the willingness of Edward Bailey to have me come. Colleagues in the Association for the Sociology of Religion, the International Conference for the Sociology of Religion, and the Society for the Scientific Study of Religion have listened and responded to the bulk of the chapters as they were presented at one or another of their meetings. A number of colleagues also shared materials with me that are not included here, and of course the book could not have appeared without the cooperation of the authors whose chapters are included. I especially appreciate Jim

Duke's preparation of the camera-ready copy for the tables and the facilities at Brigham Young University that enabled him to do so.

The year 1987 was a somewhat strange one in my life, the details of which are not particularly appropriate to recount here. Nevertheless, the support of my family, the people of St. Mark's Church, colleagues in the Association for the Sociology of Religion, and our two cats (who have been jealous ever since Tom Robbins dedicated his half of his church-state book to his) made an incredibly topsy-turvy year bearable if not enjoyable.

Religious Politics
in
Global
and
Comparative Perspective

1

The Kingdom of God and the World of Man: The Problem of Religious Politics

William H. Swatos, Jr.

It would be difficult to think of a phenomenon that caught Western students of religion more by surprise than the worldwide resurgence of religion—*political religion* no less!—that occurred with increasing visibility as the 1970s wore on. We had seen the appearance of the so-called New Religious Movements, but many of the leading theorists of religion in modernity could accommodate these into a secularization paradigm by their very bizarreness.[1] The highly eclectic character of the religious "marketplace" seemed only to confirm the privatization thesis—that religion has become a leisure time activity, with no societal consequences (except in an occasional Manson-like figure, who is more good copy than serious societal assault). Such religious controversies as did reach the press were often "explained" (i.e., explained away) by social scientists as merely symbolic expressions of socioeconomic variables (e.g., in Northern Ireland or Israel). The idea that there were concerted groups of people taking religion seriously enough to affect the order of global society gained little credence, in fact, until the appearance of the Ayatollah Khomeini in revolutionary Iran. He meant business, and the "simple" explanation that he was a mere figurehead for those "really" in power fell into greater and greater disrepute as the heads of one after another of those "really" in power rolled before Allah's revolutionary justice.

There is no weapon in the theoretical arsenal of the social scientific study of religion or of political science that can attack the problem of worldwide religious resurgence. The two primary theories of "modernization"—development or exploitation—both proceed from the assumption that religious "prejudices" hamper "progress" and are disappearing

throughout the world. Secular education, secular armies, secular economics, secular politics combine to create the modern state. The only
real difference between these two models for modernization is whether
capitalism is viewed as a friend or foe to nation-state growth and the
good order of the international system of states. According to these
theories, then, religious resurgence represents a "deviant" occurrence
in the broad sweep of history. If, indeed, only an isolated instance of
religious resurgence were to be observed, one could hardly quarrel with
such theoretical presuppositions. We have deviants intrasocietally, after
all, so why not expect the same in the international system of states?
The problem, however, is that the resurgence phenomenon is global in
character—so much so that it strains credulity to accept an argument
that it represents some form of mass delusion.

The closest social scientists have come to a systematic attempt to
account for worldwide religious resurgence is an article by Roland
Robertson and JoAnn Chirico entitled "Humanity, Globalization, and
Worldwide Religious Resurgence," published in *Sociological Analysis*
in 1985. They provide a visual model, "Trajectories of Emergence of
Humanity" (Figure 1.1), based on a contrast between "anthropocentric dualism" (the differentiation of the world into two realms: one
of "societal-systemic functionality," the other of "individual and rela-
tional being") and "global telic concern," a more holistic sense of
humanity-world interdependence. They argue "that the globality of
the resurgence of religious and quasi-religious concerns can be
understood in sociological terms only by establishing an analytical
schema which grasps the global circumstances as such and which
conceptualizes the processes yielding the evolutionary-historical thematization of humanity," or more simply, they try "to tackle the
question: *how is 'the globe' possible?*"[2]

As they see it, the linkages within the model involve "four processes
of relativization, two having to do with the relativization of societies
(trans-socialization) and two having to do with the relativization of persons, or selves (trans-personalization)." They mean by "relativization":

a process involving the placing of sociocultural or psychic entities in larger
categorical contexts, such that the relativized entities are constrained to be more
self-reflexive relative to other entities in the larger context (which does not mean
that they will actually be "constructively" self-reflexive). The relativization of
selves involves, along one dimension, the situating of selfhood in the more
inclusive and fundamental frame of what it means to be of mankind; while the
relativization of societies—along another, parallel dimension—involves the situating of concrete societies in the context of a world complex of societies—thus
constraining particular societies to judge the extent to which they exemplify
principles of "societal quality." These are the dominant processes of relativization. There branches from each a secondary process of relativization, one

Figure 1.1
Trajectories of Emergence of Humanity

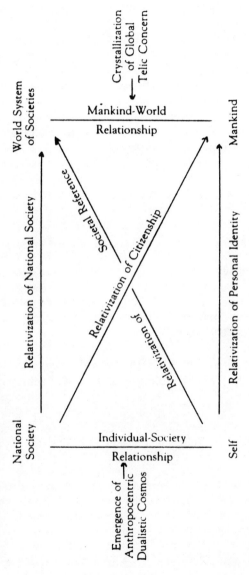

4 *William H. Swatos, Jr.*

having to do with the relationship between concrete societies and the category of man, the other involving a connection between selves and the global complex of societies.[3]

At the level of the self, "concerns with individual *being* are differentiated from *doing*," the "*relativization of personal identity*," detached from the state, leading to "a tendency toward a near-global conception of self-hood"; at the level of society, a relativization away from unilinear "*modernization*" to "a situation in which the criteria of societal change themselves are matters of inter-societal, inter-continental, inter-civilizational, and inter-doctrinal interpretation and debate."[4]

Religion enters this picture through "two features of the present global circumstance." There is, on the one hand, in the globalization process, "a 'release' from the 'security' of *life-in-society*, thus raising problems concerning both the legitimacy of *the world order of societies* and *the meaning of what mankind 'really is.'* " On the other hand, "the process of globalization does not occur without strains or discontents occurring within societies":

As globalization proceeds, pressures are exerted on societies and individuals-in-societies to define the *identity* of particular societies—a matter which analysts used to think was the special problem of *new* national societies, but which is now clearly of ubiquitous significance. At the collective-societal level there is thus a thrust in a quasi-religious direction as some take it upon themselves to define in politicoreligious terms what "their" society "ultimately stands for" and what is sacred about it.

Thus "the *conjunction* of societal civil-religion concerns *and* the incipience of *world* civil-religion problems" becomes the venue for religious politics:

Politicization of theology and religion, on the one hand, and the "theologization" of politics, on the other, are core features of this conjunction. The globalization process itself raises religious and quasi-religious questions. Theodical and eschatological questions—or successor questions to old theodical and eschatological queries—are high on the agenda of global discourse. Religion is centered in the process of globalization by virtue of both the religious or quasi-religious matters raised as a result of universalistic tendencies involving mankind and relations between societies *and* by the particularizing responses to the universalistic tendencies.[5]

That Robertson and Chirico subtitle their article "A Theoretical Exploration," and refer to their assessment of the role of religion in globalization politics as "only a *very* brief analytical prognosis," however, also make clear that more work needs to be done on this problem.[6]

During 1987, the World Society Foundation of Zürich (*Stiftung zur*

Förderung sozialwissenschaftlicher Forschung über die Weltgesellschaft) enabled me to spend a year studying value-politics in global societal perspective. I found three interrelated things to be true: First, few attempts
at global theory or research had been undertaken with respect to religious politics. Although Skocpol had years before emphasized the importance of the international system of states for understanding
intranational regime change, most studies of religious politics were case
analyses of single nation-states or were two-state comparisons.[7] That
these were often both highly informative and well written made my
reading more enjoyable, but it did not solve the larger problem. Second,
a number of the global or comparative pieces that I found most valuable
were unpublished. Third, a considerable number of these—like my own
work—were inspired by, addressed, and developed upon the Robertson-
Chirico model.

Out of these coincidences comes the present book. It contains a series
of essays addressing the worldwide politico-religious resurgence at the
global level—or at least at a level beyond the one- or two-state case
study.[8] The chapters are not intended to provide a unified theory or
definitive theoretical paradigm to explain the manifold aspects of contemporary religious politics; rather, they present a series of non–mutually exclusive accounts for these situations. The earlier chapters are
interpretive in character, focusing more closely on globalization itself as
it impacts upon culture, personality, and social structure, while those
toward the end of the book rely on quantitative comparative analyses
across a multinational spectrum. I conclude with a chapter that considers
basic questions of definition in the sociology of religion as illumined by
the phenomenon of worldwide religious politics.

Frank Lechner begins the interpretive chapters by clarifying the role
of religion in the modern world-system. He thus contributes to the
development of a non-Marxist, multidimensional world-system theory
that pays greater attention to the "cultural factor" in the process of
globalization. By analogy to Talcott Parsons's "institutionalized individualism" as definitive for liberal democratic societies, Lechner introduces
the concept of "institutionalized societalism" to emphasize the cult of
society as a constitutive symbolic element in the modern world-system.
This concept may be the most important single contribution to the development of our understanding of the underlying structures of worldwide religious resurgence. Lechner shows how intersocietal and
ostensibly antiglobal movements have important global aspects and that
various—and, in part, religious—definitions of the global situation are
part of an emerging global cultural system.

Whereas Lechner looks primarily at culture, John Simpson turns in
Chapter 3 to the concept of self in the context of globalization. Although
Simpson has reservations about the extent to which we can accurately

speak of a world or global society, he recognizes the existence of an emergent global system and wants to explore whether and how active, pragmatic self-definitions can occur within such a system and the role of religion in such definitions. He relies primarily on a Weber-like analysis to show how Calvinism resonated with nascent capitalism to underwrite the world-mastering, active self, and argues that religion in its various forms may be one product of the evolution of human species that contains elements that have the capacity to sustain meaningful action in the global context at the individual level. Simpson's chapter thus complements Lechner's emphasis on cultural systems by recognizing that globalization has consequences for the personality system as well that should not be overlooked by abstract structural analyses.

Peter Beyer, in the following chapter, provides a view of global society that may respond to Simpson's uneasiness. Explicating the work of Niklas Luhmann, Beyer argues that modern global society is characteristically not integrated by any sense of overall solidarity that includes all people, as a Parsonian interpretation might suggest, and that the development of societal inclusion should not be seen as coextensive with that of solidarities. Beyer sees solidarity as a concept that is appropriate more to the level of organizations than it is to the level of societal systems. Although the Luhmannian perspective is likely to be somewhat strange to many English-speaking readers—and it is not likely to be something many will want to swallow whole—at Beyer's hands here it nevertheless provides a marvelous tour de force in separating solidarity from society. By eliminating the very popular, but not necessarily theoretically helpful, concept of solidarity from our apparatus for conceptualizing society, Beyer frees up a new foreground for sociological approaches to religion, since the concept of solidarity has been far too central to the standard sociological conception of religion. Once we can conceive society without solidarity, we have no reason blithely to associate religion with solidarity or "integration."

My own chapter is intended to provide only a loose integration of the previous three. In it I consider, through a distinction between universalistic and particularistic ultimate values, the impact of ultimate (rather than instrumental) values in politics upon world society. The worldwide resurgence of particularistic ultimate values in politics—a variety of so-called "fundamentalisms"—is the specific problem the chapter addresses; however, I also argue that ultimate values have never been absent from politics. Instead, after World War II, universalistic ultimate values were increasingly championed by powerful nation-states. These values were functional for the development of world society, but they also enhanced the hegemony of powerful nation-states over the less powerful, and the control of more powerful intranational elites over the dispossessed. These power conflicts have set the stage for value-politics that are potentially destabilizing to world society. I use a field-theoretical approach to combine cultural, structural, and personality elements to explain the relative likelihood of the emergence and success of militant religious movements in nation-states.

In the first of the three chapters of quantitative analyses, James Duke and Barry Johnson present some of the most critical results of their massive two-hundred-nation secondary analysis of data drawn from David Barrett's *World Christian Encyclopedia* (which is, in fact, a world religions encyclopedia). By examining macrosociological data on world-wide religious change between 1900 and 1980, they provide an empirical assessment of the utility of secularization theory in explaining religious change—hence of secularization theory's underlying assumptions. They then formulate a tentative set of explanations of these changes based on this significant data analysis. Although there is no set of worldwide data on religion that is not without flaws, and all secondary analyses are limited by the lack of researcher input into the formulation of the data set, this chapter nevertheless represents an enormous advance over any previous attempt to speak authoritatively about "what is actually happening" in worldwide religious movements. It will set a standard for future research.

The following chapter, by Martha Abele Mac Iver, uses a different data set for a secondary analysis of a phenomenon she terms "religious politicization"—the self-conscious linkage made by individuals between religious beliefs and political views. Although her research is limited to European Community member nations, there is sufficient variation within this group to consider the paper world-oriented. The use of such Mediterranean states as Italy and Greece, the separation out (and inclusion) of data for Northern Ireland from those of Great Britain and of Ireland, and the inclusion of Scandinavian Denmark, as well as the central industrialized nations, show the breadth of her work. A somewhat complicated log-linear logit model (which some readers may wish to skim rather lightly) is used to investigate the determinants of religious politicization. Church membership and education are shown to be the most important predictors, after religiosity, of whether or not persons perceive their political attitudes to be influenced by their religious faith. The influence of religious politicization on particular political attitudes is then analyzed. Religiously politicized individuals are found to differ significantly from others on left-right political spectrum self-placement, views on aid to the Third World, support for the European Community, and partisan preferences, even when only the most highly religious are considered. Though the religiously politicized tend to be on the right of the party spectrum, they do hold a diversity of views. These results suggest that there are differences within individual belief systems that help to account for different ideological positions, and that as such, religion continues to be salient in predicting the political action of mass publics.

In the final substantive chapter, we return again to the work of Duke and Johnson. Here using multidata sets centered around the two-hundred nation study, they explore in a neo-Weberian analysis the relationship between religion and democracy. Specifically, they show that nation-states with a substantial Protestant heritage are more likely to be democratic than states with other religious traditions, even when level of economic development is controlled. Since it is possible, too, that initially heterogeneous societies are more likely to be democratic, and this in turn fostered the development of Protestantism, the direction of causal influence is a crucial question. By a series of statistical analyses they demonstrate that religious pluralism (and by implication social or ethnic pluralism) had no effect on the development of democratic political institutions, and by a comparison of British and French colonial state development, they show that there, too, religion had a greater influence than a specific colonial nation. They conclude, therefore, that some causal factors are present in Protestantism itself that enable Protestant nations to establish and maintain democratic political institutions more effectively than nations with other majority religions. Whereas it was suggested some years ago by Paul Honigsheim that Weber's *Protestant Ethic and the Spirit of Capitalism* was actually more concerned with politics than economics, this chapter by Duke and Johnson brilliantly revives Weber's classic on a macrosociological level.[9]

My final chapter is not intended as a summary—or "integration"—of the several chapters of the book. Each makes a unique contribution, and to try to force them into some "synthesis" would undermine their individual merits. What I have tired to do instead is suggest what *consequences* these analyses have for general theory in the sociology of religion. Beginning with a critique of secularization theory, I argue that at the root of much sociological misunderstanding of religion lies a basic flaw in the standard sociological definition of religion. This begins with problems in the work of Emile Durkheim, from which it is taken, but it is much compounded by the Parsonian-inspired functionalist adaptation of Durkheim and its perpetuation by subsequent generations of sociological theorists. I urge that the worldwide resurgence of religious politics not only requires a rethinking of "secularization," but a reconceptualization of "religion" as well. Only when this is done will the social sciences of religion be able to offer theories that predictively explain observed events.

A final word about the concept "religious resurgence" might profitably be added in concluding this chapter of introduction to the problems of contemporary religious politics. The sociological classics of Weber and Durkheim both identify religion with morality. In this sense, at least, they remain theoretically timely for the present day. The worldwide religious resurgence is as significant as it is because it is a resurgence of religion-based moralities. It is not at all clear that participants in the religious resurgence as we have observed it are more theologically so-phisticated than other religious believers. Indeed, in all the major cases of resurgence, the doctrinal content of the movement is heterodox or heretical. In no case does resurgence leadership represent the leadership of the predominant expressions of any world religion. In cases where we have credible statistics, furthermore, such as Northern Ireland or the United States, the number of core adherents to resurgence movements (e.g., Paisley's own denomination, the Moral Majority, and so on), are very small compared to their political peripheries.[10] What the "religious resurgence" represents, then, wherever it occurs, is an attempt to im-plement a moral agenda on a mass public that is presumed to share certain general cultural orientations and personal and societal experi-ences with a militant core of religious virtuosi. The inability of main-stream political leaders to articulate a clear value position for their actions and to yield benefits on a broad basis for their constituencies creates the potential void into which these movements can step. The primary reason why the sociology of religion is the most potentially useful vehicle for theoretical analyses of these movements is its recognition that religious doctrine cannot be severed from religious practice and that religious practice by groups takes on far greater significance in any society than the mere sum of its individual members may suggest.

2

Cultural Aspects of the Modern World-System

Frank J. Lechner

A century ago, the challenge for the scholars who were to become the "classical" sociologists was to make sense of the great transformation in the European societies of their time. They founded the sociological tradition by formulating two core problems: the (analytical) problem of social order and the (historical) problem of modernity. These were related. Determining how social order is possible in general may (and did) tell us something about how it is possible under particular conditions—for example, after a period of radical change. Determining the distinctive character and origins of this new form of social order, modernity, may (and did) raise questions about conventional accounts of social order. The tradition is alive and well. Their problems are our problems still.

But today this tradition is undergoing significant change. If traditions may be distinguished by the core problems they address, we can say that the sociological one is now changing its identity by the development of new core problems: the problems of global order and globality.[1] They are as profound as those of the classics. They are pushing the discipline in a new direction, while in part they subsume the older problems. But we have not yet developed a way of dealing with these problems that is theoretically satisfactory and can serve as the late-twentieth-century equivalent of the classical contributions. The question, then, is how we can do for the globe what the classical sociologists did for society. In this chapter I draw on the classical tradition, represented by Durkheim, Weber, and Simmel, to clarify the current global challenge in sociology and to make some theoretical and substantive contributions. In doing so it will also become a little clearer where we need to go beyond the classics.

Let us first compare the different problems with which the classics and we are dealing. Just as their theoretical work was rooted in a basic awareness that they were living in a new *Gesellschaft*-like society, so the new core problems spring from a basic awareness among contemporary sociologists that we are now living in a truly global society, in a *world-system*.[2] We live in one world economy and in one system of multiple but interacting states. We have become conscious of the world as one social arena, in which we are exposed continuously to the points of view of others. We know how this has been made possible by technological innovations in communication and transportation. At the very least, global interdependence has intensified substantially. New institutions connect different parts of the globe. And there is a pattern, a certain order, to the new global condition. We are witnessing the *Vergesells-chaftung* of the globe. But what exactly is the nature, and what are the origins, of this particular world order? And how is any global order possible in principle? These are the new core questions.

Like the social condition studied by the classics, ours is not completely unprecedented. After all, medieval Christianity was a religious world-system, encompassing and linking many communities. The historic empires integrated communities across vast areas into one political and sometimes cultural framework. The modern world-system obviously is historically linked to, and still preserves some of the features of, the economic networks of early capitalism and the system of European states. So ours is not the first "world" system, although its worldliness is now coextensive with the globe itself, the infrastructure for globality is more solid than in any previous era, and more aspects of life are now globally integrated than ever before. The problem remains to determine the extent and the nature of the discontinuity.

The classical problem of modernity is the problem of a particular historical transformation. It refers to a qualitative break in social relationships. It has a temporal reference. It is located in a particular civilizational context, even though, as Robertson has shown, the classics had some awareness of global issues.[3] The problem of globality, on the other hand, is not simply the problem of a transformation over time, but above all of a transformation in the scale of social life. It has a spatial reference. But it is not located within any particular civilization; rather, it is the problem of the coexistence and interaction of multiple civilizations in a common context. The classical problem could be handled by historical and comparative methods; today these approaches may no longer suffice. To be adequate to the new global task, the sociological tradition may well have to develop a new set of general methods.[4]

Though the classics did not operate in an intellectual vacuum, they still had to generate most of their own theoretical resources. In studying the modern world-system we certainly do not have to start from scratch.

We have a century of sociology behind us. In this respect our situation is obviously different from that of the classics. We can stand on their shoulders, not simply because they were giants who came before us, but because our new problems include important elements of theirs. Strictly speaking, the "problem of global order" is not a neatly analytical one, since it rather concretely refers to the globe. But then the old problem of social order was not purely analytical either: it was a question of societal order, though dealt with in abstractly analytical terms. Thus, insofar as they solved the problem of social order, we should be able to incorporate the results of the classics in our own work. Similarly, the problem of globality, of the nature and origins of the modern world-system, obviously includes the question of modernity—it is the problem of the globalization of societal modernity. Thus we should be able to use the traditional analyses of *Gesellschaft*, while recognizing the points at which our problems require different solutions. The classics also pointed the way to a certain type of theory that has proved useful. We should preserve it if we can. Finally, the classics showed that any social order is contingent, that it could be otherwise, that it is one possible world among many. Similarly, the modern world-system is only one possible form of world order, conventionally characterized as one world economy with multiple polities and cultures. It is a particular selection under particular constraints from many objectively possible arrangements. This is what institutionalization is all about. To think of globalization, the process by which the modern world-system took form, as a process of institutionalization is another lesson to be drawn from the classical tradition.[5] The question, of course, is whether institutionalization on a global scale is in some way radically different from societal institutionalization as it has been conceived heretofore.

Having formulated some fundamental problems as a "prolegomenon to any future globology" by comparison with classical problems, I will focus in the remainder of this chapter on some relatively neglected aspects of world-system analysis.

REVISIONISM IN WORLD-SYSTEM THEORY

The classics shared a common set of problems. They also formulated, in spite of many substantive disagreements, the essentials of a new theoretical method. While we do not have to accept Parsons's convergence thesis about the classical treatment of action and order,[6] it remains reasonable to see in their works the outline of a voluntaristic or "multidimensional" theory, to use Jeffrey Alexander's somewhat problematic term.[7] Sidestepping the many debates about divergences among the classical authors, I will assume for the purposes of this analysis that there is a classical theoretical method or "logic." My point is that this sets some minimal standards by which world-system theory should be measured, unless it can be shown that the latter requires a fundamentally different kind of theoretical approach.

There are many forms of world-system analysis, but there is one hegemonic world-system theory, namely Immanuel Wallerstein's, which incorporates elements of previous theories of macrolevel change. This hegemony is now being challenged, however, in ways similar to the classical critique of utilitarian and one-sided accounts of action and order. Although Wallerstein's work has been vigorously criticized on many substantive points, it still stands as the most influential "model" of the world-system.[8] Paying attention to a body of theory that is in many respects false is justified because the critical reactions tell us something about the proper way to deal with the new twin problems of sociology. They point the way to a theoretical method that satisfies the classical standards.

The classics dealt in different ways, first, with the utilitarian dilemma.[9] How does one account for order if one starts from the assumption of self-interested, autonomous actors who somehow rationally engage in interaction? This cannot be done on strictly utilitarian grounds. According to Bergesen, Wallerstein's theorizing resembles nineteenth-century utilitarianism insofar as interaction between parts—the characteristics of which can be determined independently—is presumed to account for the global whole.[10] Particular countries have certain strengths and weaknesses, on the basis of which they engage in exchange, out of which emerges a global division of labor, in which different countries play different roles. Small initial differences, filtered through interaction on the world market, produce large consequences. Once the structure is established, to be sure, there is a certain continuity to it; for example, the core-periphery structure remains even though different countries may occupy the positions. But the argument essentially treats countries (their dominant elites) as rational actors with given interests and with certain resources at their disposal.

Just as the sociological paradigm transcended the utilitarian tradition by emphasizing the primacy of structural properties of societal wholes, so, according to Bergesen, world-system theory needs to become a form of "globology" in order to establish the fact that the global whole is more than the sum or interaction of its parts. Globology is to focus on the systemic features of world order as such. This holistic move is appropriate, but it has certain limitations. For one thing, as recent reevaluations of the classical tradition suggest, the theory program inherent in the "sociological paradigm" is not merely holistic.[11] It also emphasizes the continuing interpenetration of action and order, and of parts and wholes. This is a matter of what Alexander has called theoretical logic, not of substantive theory. But it is relevant to the latter. It tells us that models of the "world-system" cannot simply be formulated in structural terms; they must contain variables that account for (at least the existence of) parts of or particular entities within the system. Bergesen's suggestion that global order can be equated with a particular global mode of production does not explain the nature and role of parts (e.g., class actors) as such, and thus suffers from what might be called holistic reductionism.

Wallerstein's theory, as it stands, is an essentially materialistic theory, although it does not require a simple form of determinism, and it is not a one-factor theory. In light of the classical model, this is a problem. Order comes about, to use a bit of jargon, through the interpenetration of "conditioning" and "controlling" dimensions of a system. Again, this is a matter of theoretical logic rather than substantive theory. But it tells us that Bergesen's counterproposal is not sufficient. It remains trapped in the utilitarian dilemma by accounting for order in terms of structural constraint on the behavior of actors.[12] And after all, Durkheim's point about precontractual elements in contract did not merely suggest that we should look for deep-structural economic variables, as Bergesen seems to interpret it in relation to global class structure, but that any account of rational economic action must necessarily involve a set of guiding (not "determining") normative elements. The code behind unequal exchange cannot be reduced to a particular type of class structure.

So globology must be holistic, but not too much, and pay attention to normative patterns, but without simply turning conventional materialism on its head. Other revisionists have gone beyond Wallerstein in yet another way by pointing to analytical dimensions of the world-system that he underestimated or "reduced" to economic requirements of the system. True, Wallerstein has paid substantial attention to the role of states and has come to qualify his early view of the epiphenomenal status of culture, but the revisions argue for a more considerable change in perspective. Thus we find in Modelski's work an effort to develop a "political" world-system theory, in which the actions and interactions of political actors develop and change a transsocietal order.[13] Zolberg, who in other respects disagrees with Modelski, has also put forth a thesis of the prior existence of a world-system of states to modify Wallerstein's view of the world economy.[14] In a later contribution Zolberg takes the interpenetration of economic, political, and cultural variables largely for granted, while criticizing the very attempt to conceptualize a world "system."[15] Meyer and his associates have called attention to the role of a world polity as the legitimating cultural context in which particular political entities may function.[16] Finally, Wuthnow has attempted to "bring the cultural factor back in" by relating cultural developments and movements to trends in the world economy; he also has pointed to contributions of cultural movements to world order per se.[17] But in spite of such advances, revisionism has not produced a full-fledged theory. Global sociology is still in its infancy. Yet our picture of the globe has been enriched, and the developing theory is becoming more and more "multidimensional."

INSTITUTIONALIZED SOCIETALISM

One of the puzzles confronting the classical sociologists was the peculiar presence of "the individual" in the new *Gesellschaft*-like society. They had to produce a nonindividualistic theory of this new social order that would also account for individualism and individuation as social facts. We face an analogous puzzle today in the form of the empirical existence of independent societies in the new world-system. We have to produce a non- or transsocietal theory that also accounts for this peculiar fact. It must be a theory of a world-system that ensures the viability of societies as interdependent but relatively autonomous units. To be sure, the modern world-system is more than an aggregate of societies, just as the classical *Gesellschaft* was more than an association of individuals. Yet one of its constitutive features is that it is a "*Gesellschaft* of *Gesellschafts*," and thus the presence of societies as constituent elements in the world-system is a global fact that any adequate globology must address.

Certain solutions to the puzzle are not acceptable in light of the guidelines of the previous section. One could argue, for example, that societies make a functional contribution to the global system. One world society would be hard to manage; decentralization works better. This is a form of functional segmentation that has its origins in the previous European system of states. But functional necessity by itself, even if it could be convincingly demonstrated, is not enough: Why should the performance of functions take this particular form and remain stable over time? How is the performance of these functions perceived and evaluated by actors on the global scene? Utilitarian answers are as inadequate as purely functional ones. "International relations" as a theoretical perspective is the global equivalent of societal utilitarianism. It presupposes the existence of separate, independent units with given interests and calculable rules by which to enter into contractual (or conflictual) relationships. The nation-state appears, in both realist and world-system theory, as an objectively existing, rational, functional actor on the global scene, operating under external systemic constraints. But why should the nation-state be the relevant actor, and what counts as societal rationality in the global context? What are the precontractual elements in transsocietal relationships and the preconflictual elements in global conflicts? This remains unclear in all forms of global utilitarianism.

The classical heuristic guidelines, on the other hand, suggest that we look for the emergence of global value standards in terms of which particular societies can construct and legitimate their identities. Maintaining a world-system of societies involves a global search for the legitimate terms of existence of particular societies and for shared criteria to evaluate proper societal functioning. At the same time, particular societies do not just operate as global actors but should be found to formulate their particular identities more explicitly and justify them in more transsocietal terms. This does not mean that we simply turn to an idealist explanation of why societies "exist" at all. The point here is simply that a world-*system* of societies requires normative elements, however problematic their status may be, to complement merely functional organization. Idealism would mean theoretical regression by classical criteria. Thus we cannot simply postulate a global "common culture" that somehow guarantees global order. But we can and should look for the essential ways in which the "ultimate" problems, such as the nature and role of constituent elements, of this sociocultural order are "thematized," if only to determine the terms in which global conflict will take place.

My specific substantive suggestion in this regard may be seen as a "Durkheimian" contribution to world-system theory. For Durkheim the problem was to find an object of commonality in an increasingly functionally differentiated type of system. Individualism in a merely utilitarian sense was for him only part of the problem, insofar as it could not provide the basis for empirical integration. The cult of the individual, however, could be shared by participants in widely different spheres; it could provide a basis of solidarity and legitimate differentiation and personal autonomy. The cult of the individual was an emerging property of a particular type of society and thus a social fact. Personhood and individual rights were established not only as a matter of principle but came also to be anchored in an institutional framework. This is a theme that runs through Parsons's work; he termed it "institutionalized individualism."

I suggest, with some qualifications, that the situation in the modern world-system is structurally similar. The problem is to find a plausible object of commonality, in a differentiated system with many apparently independent units, that can serve as a basis for empirical integration. The analogy with Durkheim's cult of the individual suggests part of the answer: a core element of the emerging global culture is the cult of the nation-state, or what I will call "institutionalized societalism." By this I mean something more than the mere existence of nation-states as functional units, just as Durkheim was referring to more than individualism or the mere existence of empirical individuals as rational actors. Rather, the concept denotes the *cult* of the nation-state—the way in which the nation-state has become both an ultimate symbol and an institutionalized global norm. Just as "the individual" in Durkheim's sense was a social fact, "society" in my sense is a global fact. "Society" has thus become more than a political entity with specific self-interests, or a moral community to which members can become subjectively attached. More than a self-sufficient unit within a larger system, it has become one of the foci of global culture. This is not to say that every particular society as such is globally valued—just as in Durkheim the cult of the individual does not imply that every individual somehow has moral standing. However, as an ultimate symbol with global-institutional backing, it does provide normative anchorage for all particular societies irrespective of their internal functioning.

One hundred years ago there were few full-fledged societies. Now there are more than a hundred and fifty. The globe is covered by state-organized societies, with distinct boundaries and cultures, that control territories, include a full complement of institutions, and structure the lives of citizens. After World War II, the sanctity of societal life was elevated to the level of High Principle and Ultimate Symbol. Societal existence is a thing set apart, held sacred. It has the symbolic trappings of the sacred. It is an object of ultimate concern, worth dying for. Once "born," a society will be treated as if it will continue forever. A properly constituted society has eternal life on earth. Even small and fragile entities such as Luxembourg, once formed and recognized, persist as symbolic entities. This sanctity of societal life also implies ultimate legitimation for societal self-defense. Where societal existence is perceived to be at stake, total conflict becomes legitimate. All resources—cultural, social, personal, technical—can, even must, be mobilized in such cases. Just as institutionalized individualism is an important preconflictual element in intrasocietal conflict, institutionalized societalism has become a condition for regional or global conflict. While human rights figure prominently in current global discourse, societal rights actually have gained priority. They are what people are expected to live and die for. While species survival is becoming an important element in global discourse on nuclear war, it has to compete with claims on behalf of societal survival. In the present global condition, species survival without societal survival is thus almost meaningless.

Like all ultimate symbols and highly general values, societalism can be interpreted and justified in different ways, just as the old individualism left a lot of room for societal variations and individual experimentation. Thus "societies" can be variously seen, from the point of view of different global actors, as the necessary embodiments of particular historical traditions, locked in ineradicable conflict, or as universalistic entities, participating in a global revolution leading to world government, or as entities charged with a global and conciliatory mission. All societies are carriers of values and of rights. But their conceptions of their global roles are clearly highly variable. Institutionalized societalism does not specify the "identity" of particular societies either. Different types of societal experiments—from open egalitarian to closed hierarchical—are possible as long as minimal criteria of proper societal competence are met. Societal incompetence becomes the agreed-upon (but obviously hard-to-define-and-implement) basis for exclusion from the world community. Lebanon may be a case in point.

By analogy with the inclusion of individual members as citizens in a legally organized societal community, the institutionalization of societalism is expressed in the inclusion of societies in the world community on an equal basis, with equal protection under international law and the one-country-one-vote policy of the United Nations General Assembly (though one member has three votes). This means, first of all, that in order to qualify for membership in the world-system one must constitute oneself as a society—with a properly organized state, a range of relevant institutions, and the necessary symbolic trappings.

There is only this one legitimate global model for the organization of social life. This model has constrained even the actions of elites attempting to break away from what they perceive as Western political and cultural domination. In addition, rules for (inter)societal behavior have been elaborated in recent decades—for example, through the growth of international law, the conventions on human rights, and the Vienna convention on treaties.[18] International law and the Charter of the United Nations put special emphasis on the inviolability of the rights, property, and territory of nations. The obvious problems in backing such global norms with authoritative sanctions, a characteristic of institutionalization within properly constituted societies, suggests that institutionalizing societalism is obviously harder than institutionalizing individualism.

This argument about institutionalized societalism can be used to "postdict" Boli-Bennett's well-known finding of convergence across societies on a transnational ideology of state authority, as reflected in the form and content of constitutions.[19] In his interpretation, this ideology reflects and supports the competitive nature of the state system in which particular nation-states can serve as vehicles for status competition and ideological competition among elites. Why the system should be multicentered, or why elite competition should take this particular form, is essentially left unexplained. Such underlying questions can be answered more readily from the perspective of institutionalized societalism.

The argument thus far has been that the modern world-system is in part a system of societies, rooted in the common, global, sacred conception of the "society" as the ultimately desirable form of social existence, one that has been institutionalized around the globe. This argument is open to several objections. First, it seems to imply that any collectivity that satisfies the minimal criteria of the global model of society qualifies as a full member of the system. However, there appear to be exceptions to the rule. South Vietnam and Hong Kong are cases in point: societies that have disappeared or will do so. On the other hand, there are collectivities, such as the Palestinians, that possess many of the required characteristics yet are not recognized as full-fledged societies. Finally, there are now many types of organizations and associations that are transsocietal. The flows of material and symbolic resources hardly respect societal boundaries anymore, if ever they did, and so the functional importance of societies may have declined, presumably undermining the symbolic value attached to them.

But do these "exceptions" require modification of the argument? I do not think so. There are very few societies that once qualified as such and have ceased to exist, and those that did were in ambiguous positions to begin with. Perhaps the best example is the incorporation of the Baltic states into the Soviet Union, which indeed was a violation of a basic global norm—but can be recognized as such only because the norm is in fact a powerful one. The exceptions to the rule are in fact exceptional. Moreover, the fact that worthy aspirants to societal status do not receive recognition is not a counterargument. Their very aspirations confirm the power of the global model. In principle, the exclusion of potential members is a natural complement of the inclusion of existing societies and a necessary element of global boundary maintenance. Finally, the growing importance of transsocietal bonds, dependent as they are on societal contributions, does not affect our current societalism directly. Certainly intersocietal integration remains extremely problematic, even where "objectively" such association might be quite beneficial—such as the case of the Organization for African Unity. "Mere" nationalism and divergence of interests are only part of the problem; fundamental integration is blocked as long as an ultimate symbolic premium exists on the maintenance of societyhood. Altruistic societal suicide—say, by the Netherlands in the interest of European integration—cannot be legitimate, since it undermines a primary principle in the interest of a secondary one.[20]

Second, it could be argued that this is essentially an idealistic argument about a global normative structure that has little relevance to the facts of global life. Consider only two of the seemingly most pressing global problems: violence and inequality. The norms of societalism do not seem to prevent extreme violence. The inclusion of societies as equal members in a world-system does not seem to move them toward actual equality. But these points can also be refuted. Clearly, if global conflict were to escalate and lead to either the obliteration of a large number of societies (or the species itself), institutionalized societalism would disappear. But the mere fact of conflict does not signal the absence of norms—any more than it does in respect to the presence of personal violence in the context of the institutionalized individualism of liberal democratic societies. Moreover, institutionalized societalism is the very basis for most conflicts—for defining the actors engaged in the conflict, the interests at stake, the ultimate objectives of the parties, and the accepted modes of conflict resolution. Similarly, institutionalized societalism establishes a measure of equality and makes units comparable in the first place; it is a basis for claims for societal respect and rewards. Rather than establishing a preconceived symbolic hierarchy, it allows a functional or historically based hierarchy to emerge. Institutionalized societalism does imply the norm that societies, as part of their proper functioning and as a test of their competence, engage in intersocietal prestige competition.[21] Thus we can reason by analogy with Marshall's argument at the global level that societal equality-in-principle, like the equality of citizenship, in fact legitimates forms of "class" inequality.[22] Global inequality becomes problematic precisely in light of global standards concerning the quality of societal life.

MOVEMENTS

The classical conception of order was not that of a seamless web of human relationships, of a smoothly functioning social organism. Modernity, in particular, was seen as a form of social order subject to all kinds of tensions. The sociological tradition tells us that in any type of sociocultural system, especially those in the process of formation, order is likely to be problematic and contentious. This classical heuristic can be applied to the world-system as well. In the process of globalization a new form of global order emerges, based on "presuppositions" like the one discussed in the previous section and subject to distinct tensions. Although there is an overarching system and an emerging culture, we would expect to find different definitions of the global situation. By analogy with collective action at the societal level, we would expect those who most experience the discontents of globalization to engage in efforts to resolve in radical fashion fundamental problems inherent in globalization. The mere fact of global interdependence is one such problem; so is the exposure of every particular society to the ideological challenge of others in almost permanent intercivilizational encounters.[23] The institutionalization of such encounters is itself likely to become a part of global culture, but the point here is that they involve a global "struggle of the gods." The problem of modernity is thus exacerbated.

Reasoning by analogy to a classical example may again provide a useful starting point. Weber analyzed religious traditions as different forms of world rejection dealing with similar problems (of salvation and theodicy, above all) in increasingly complex societies. Now the challenge is to chart the various forms of (more concrete and not necessarily transcen-

dent) world rejection, dealing with a common global condition on the
basis of different traditions and different positions in the world-system.[24]
Just as modernity produced various forms of "antimodern movements,"[25] so globalization produces different, radically critical responses,
which Wallerstein has called "antisystemic movements."[26] Recognizing
that globalization involves the institutionalization of some common "metaphysical presuppositions" around the globe, he has acknowledged the
possibility of different kinds of fundamental challenges to this process.
The task now is to analyze the forms these challenges are likely to take.[27]
I suggest that they are in part extensions of earlier antimodern movements, value-oriented efforts to reconstruct the globe in a dedifferentiating fashion and subject to similar internal dilemmas and problems
of institutionalization.

If we want to chart forms of world rejection and antisystemic collective
action, we need to know what is being rejected and challenged. What
kind of global order is emerging in the late twentieth century? Although
theories differ on the exact dynamics of the system, there is widespread
agreement on the existence of one capitalist world economy, with one
global division of labor. Clearly we also have one world polity, albeit
one consisting of multiple bureaucratic states and thus highly decen-
tralized. In addition, there is now one pluralistic world culture, not in
the sense that there is a global consensus on matters of ultimate value,
but in the sense that actors in different parts of the system share at least
some conceptions about what the world is like and what is worth striving
for. Finally, we might add that this is also a world-system consisting of
multiple communities and life worlds, multiple solidarities within and
across societal boundaries.

This one world economy and one world culture with multiple states
and life worlds forms a hierarchical and differentiated system. The hierarchy, obvious in different kinds of inequality, is one of the main
themes in conventional world-system analysis. Without elaborating on
this in any way, the point is that patterns of inequality, once delegiti-
mated, become powerful sources of antisystemic action. Furthermore,
economic, political, social, and cultural aspects of the system are likely
to crystallize independently—and have done so in the past. Of course,
this does not mean that there are no historical or functional connections
between the spheres. Such connections, in the form of what Münch has
called "interpenetration," were crucial to the classical analysis of differentiation.[28] They are crucial for the analysis of global differentiation as
well, though of course to spell this out would require writing an alternative world history. The main point here is that, if a system undergoes
differentiation or develops in a differentiated fashion, the functioning
of different spheres and the interests of major collectivities in those
spheres become relatively autonomous. This implies that there is room

for different ideological challengers, especially since global culture becomes an autonomous domain in its own right. On the other hand, we
can expect close correlations between cultural parties and actors in other
domains to be the exception rather than the rule. Cultural alliances can
be expected to be increasingly differentiated from economic or political
alliances, and thus no longer tied to class-based collective action—a
phenomenon noted by Wallerstein that can be explained by a form of
global differentiation theory.[29]

Thus we have a differentiated and hierarchically organized system. It
is also a pluralistic or "open" one.[30] For even if we assume, with Wallerstein, that there are global "metaphysical presuppositions" (such as
universalism and rationalism), which presumably are the result of cultural penetration of the periphery by the core, such presuppositions
necessarily remain general and abstract, and any abstract principles can
be interpreted in many different ways—hence their manifestations in
different societal contexts are likely to vary significantly. For example,
there is no universal interpretation of universalism. Precisely because
of the relative abstractness of current global culture, different kinds of
challenges to seemingly dominant Western bourgeois presuppositions
become possible, challenges that are unlikely to be constrained by a
minimal common culture that has little controlling influence. Thus, while
there may be such a minimal common global culture, strengthened by
the globalization of science and of "consumer culture," this global culture is an "open" one. This openness is linked to institutionalized societalism: If societal autonomy is globally legitimated as a ground rule
in global cultural conflict and if societies are globally defined as institutional carriers of value, then comparisons between societies, debates
about their internal functioning, and competitions of ideologies can be
expected. Institutionalized societalism makes possible society-based
movements challenging other societies. Just as in the Parsonian view of
the "open" society institutionalized individualism is a condition for, or
at least a correlate of, a critically rational and pluralistic culture, so institutionalized societalism as a global fact can be seen as a necessary
condition for a critical, open, global culture. Societies, to put it meta-
phorically, become like active (though, unfortunately, armed) denominations—in spite of the desires of some to operate as sects or churches.[31]

If what has been said above gives a reasonable, albeit obviously se-
lective, descriptive account of the direction of globalization and its re-
sulting world-system, how can a good world-system theory chart the
directions of world rejection and identify characteristic problems and
unintended consequences that different approaches to the globe are
likely to have? As I suggested above, an extension of a model developed
for societal antimodern movements provides a useful approach, though
this does not imply that "societal" analysis holds the key to our global

problems. In earlier work I have argued that modernity produces certain basic types of discontents that become the focus of radical forms of value-oriented, dedifferentiating collective action.[32] The same can be argued with respect to globalization. The perceived discontents of modernity are exacerbated. Actors operating from different traditions and positions in the world-system formulate radical counterimages to the hierarchical, differentiated, and pluralistic system that has resulted from Western expansion. Even movements dealing with societal discontents are increasingly drawn into global projects.

As a first case in point, consider Marxist-inspired movements. To be sure, their fortunes have been on the wane, and the societies that until recently defined themselves as the carriers of alternative values, as the pioneers of a different kind of world-system, are now undergoing great changes. Empirically, then, it is not clear how vigorous antisystemic movements of the Marxist variety will be in the near future. I earlier characterized them as "Promethean" efforts to reconstruct a meaningful order through dedifferentiation on the basis of adaptation as a value principle oriented more concretely toward human emancipation.[33] The intellectual image of the world on which Promethean-type movements relied has always been that of a world-system—something that can be traced to Marx's own work. At the global level such Promethean efforts logically focus on the discontents produced by the exploitative nature of the world economy and its distortion of man's true nature. The corresponding emancipatory view of the globe will focus on man's capacity for creative world mastery through a change in the global mode of production. Relativizing the alienating societal restrictions on that creativity and attacking the global class structure, the liberation based on insight into man's true interest is in principle a universalistic enterprise, based on a universalistic conceptual framework. In the modern world-system, liberation has to mean more than transcending societal exploitation; it means using, as a temporary device, the apparatus of different states to express the interests of the globally oppressed, to create a division of labor in which all individuals can develop their capacities to the fullest, to restore the communities of those who have suffered from Western domination, and to undermine Western bourgeois cultural hegemony.

This Marxist-inspired view of the global condition has been quite influential in both theory and praxis. However, its institutionalization has proved difficult. As ideology, it incorporated much of bourgeois thought, including its universalism and its emphasis on world mastery, which undermined its capacity for radical critique. In practice, the class base for a global emancipatory movement failed to crystallize early in this century; the socialism-in-one-country strategy meant the beginning of a process of partial co-optation. The well-known failures of movements

nominally committed to class emancipation in carrying out their policies
fatally weakened their efforts at the global level. But this does not mean
that no change has been achieved, since at the very least the balance of
wealth and power between different sectors of the world-system has
changed since the beginning of this century and the radical view of
global emancipation remains a strong ideological challenge to main-
stream globalization.

A different kind of challenge stems from a collectivist kind of roman-
ticism, a dedifferentiating effort on the basis of the value of integration,
advocating communal closure, and rejecting the universalistic and differentiating thrust of global *Gesellschaft*.[34] Attacking both functional differentiation and an enlightened global culture in the name of a vision
of a close, solidary *Gemeinschaft*, this romantic effort is particularistic.
States should represent communities, cultures express communal identities, economies nurture communal solidarity. The focus is on the res-
toration of solidarity, especially of the ethnic kind. Economic resources,
state bureaucracies, and appeals to common global principles like nationalism should be used to convert the globe into a system of coexisting
and mutually exclusive communities.

Of course, ethnic antisystemic movements, which vary considerably
in their practical objectives and societal circumstances, also have had
great difficulties in institutionalizing their global visions. National liberation movements inspired by visions of close communal solidarity,
once successful, often gave up what little was left of a specific ethnic
ideological inspiration. Ethnic movements striving for recognition
adopted many common features of the world-system—the appeals to
nationalism, the demand for independent statehood, and the like. Moreover, institutionalized societalism proved a difficult barrier to overcome—movements had to work within the framework of established
states, seemingly an "iron cage" into which their leadership was co-
opted. Furthermore, in spite of considerable global variation in conceptions of solidarity, the universalistic thrust of globalization has proved
hard to dislodge, in part because it is a universalism that leaves room
for and in fact legitimates, within limits, particular attachments to particular communities. Still, the movements have changed the world system somewhat, since at the very least they were part of the "revolt
against the West" and as such have added to global pluralism.[35]

Perhaps most important among the antisystemic movements is the
new fundamentalism, especially in Islamic countries.[36] Fundamentalist
efforts at reconstruction of a meaningful order are a form of dedifferentiation based on absolute dedication to maintenance of a particular
value pattern. At the global level, the thrust of fundamentalism is to
attempt to restructure the globe in terms of a particular set of value
principles and relativize existing cultural traditions and societies on that

basis. Rejecting pluralistic and disenchanted global *Gesellschaft*, this fundamentalist effort, in principle covering all dimensions of global life, is both hierarchical and universalistic. On the basis of a properly restored global culture, the other spheres can be restored as well, with the economy subject to religious principles, communities based on a brotherhood of faith, and states implementing religiously inspired programs. After a successful Islamic revolution, the globe is intended to become a common religious civilization.

Like antisystemic movements of the Marxist variety, fundamentalist movements have had some success in particular societies, especially Iran. The inspiration is profound, the message is coherent, the available resources are considerable, and the movement is only in its early stages. It will gain strength in the years to come. In spreading the Islamic revolution, however, fundamentalists will run into several problems. Not only is the Islamic community internally divided, but support for fundamentalist actions is also often not religiously based and is likely to decline as fundamentalists gain in worldly influence. The very effort to restore a tradition is a modern thing to do; in implementing a "cultural" program, fundamentalists are forced into accommodation with the economic and political structures of the modern world-system. Differentiation and secularity in a global culture are even harder to undo at the global level than they are at the societal level; hence fundamentalists cannot succeed on their own terms. Still, they can add a "fundamentally" new component to global culture and change the economic and political balance in the world—and in fact have done so.

My argument has been that in the process of globalization there emerge several types of antisystemic movements that challenge some central features of the world-system, that are made possible by this same world-system, and that can be analyzed at least in part by extending a model developed for a societal-level analysis of antimodern movements. This extension obviously has been sketched here only in general terms. Several problems remain unsolved. For example, in spite of Wuthnow's pioneering work on the relationship between movements and world-system dynamics, we are in only the early stages of identifying such links and accounting for the global fate of movements with global aspirations. These aspirations, rooted in distinct forms of "world rejection," are themselves only in the process of crystallization and thus less tangible than "objective" features of the world economy (and as a result may have been underemphasized by Wuthnow).[37] In addition, while the global shift in movement analysis is theoretically and empirically justified, the relationship between global-level and societal-level forces is still unclear. Finally, while there are good theoretical grounds for distinguishing between four elementary forms of societal antimodern movements, no such claim seems justified at the global level. The examples discussed above, at least, do not exhaust the possibilities of antisystemic activity. For example, it could be argued that the worldwide environmental movement belongs in this category, as do religious collectivities that operate outside normal societal channels to promote an alternative view of the world-system. Among the latter are the Roman Catholic Church and the Unification Church. To analyze all of these is beyond the bounds of this chapter. They should be the focus of a developing sociology of world culture.

CONCLUSION

After arguing that the sociological tradition is going through an important transition because of a change in its core problems, I suggested that in order to deal with the new problems of global order and globality a type of theory is required that satisfies the basic classical standards. Under the influence of revisionist world-system analysis, this is now beginning to be developed. As substantive contributions to this line of work, I proposed, first, that a crucial component of the modern world-system is "institutionalized societalism," and second, that in the process of globalization radical types of antisystemic movements challenge some essential features of the emerging world-system on the basis of alternative images of the globe. These can be seen as "Durkheimian" and "Weberian" proposals, respectively.

Apart from theoretical and, more important, empirical problems pertaining to the substantive proposals—the analysis is intended as the foundation for further work—the unresolved issue adumbrated in this chapter is, of course, the major one, namely the problem of global order itself. If the problem has a "solution" at all, it should be one that avoids the mistakes of the past, by treating order neither as the result of forceful constraint and rational action nor as the result of natural solidarity rooted in common ultimate values. It should be a solution that plausibly accounts for the main features of the actually existing, hierarchical, differentiated, and highly pluralistic world order. In looking for the global forms that structure our diverse experiences, positions, and orientations in the complex global arena, perhaps we ultimately will find a Simmelian solution.[38]

3

Globalization, the Active Self, and Religion: A Theory Sketch

John H. Simpson

In coming to theoretical grips with modern global circumstances and the roles of religions in the processes of globalization, where and how does one "cut into the cake," so to speak, in order to construct an interpretive understanding that has sociological integrity? This question is not a simple one to answer primarily because the major theoretical paradigms used by sociologists to account for society and social life assume a focusing mechanism or settled structure that is supposed to solve the problem of order. Contemporary neo-Marxian theoretical discourse, for example, assumes the existence of the state (if only in a negative or critical sense), while action theory posits an integrated social system. Those assumptions, clearly, are not applicable to the globe as a singular unit.

It may not be possible to construct a grand theory of the globe because the order of complexity of the emergent global system may not *in principle* be reducible to the forms of discourse that attract the label of "adequate theory." Thus, any extension of either neo-Marxian or action theory or any other type of theory to the global level of analysis may run the risk of being simply ideology and rhetoric to the extent that it is claimed that an adequate and complete theoretical description of structures and processes exists. The notion of the possibility of a grand theory of the globe can, then, be questioned on two grounds: (1) a theoretically palpable empirical focus of order—a state or integrated social system—does not exist at the global level, and (2) emergent complexity undermines any claim that a theory is, in fact, complete and adequate.

It is not the purpose of this chapter to develop an argument that leads directly to the conclusions put forward in the preceding paragraph. Such an argument would, indeed, constitute a kind of theory—albeit not in the classical theoretical mold—of globalization. Rather, I want to enlarge upon what has elsewhere been described as a "theory sketch" of the emergent global situation.[1] A theory sketch of or perspective on the global situation begins with the recognition of incompleteness in the sense that all discourse within the perspective is conditioned by the notion that statements are limited in their descriptive and analytic adequacy by the complexity of the emergent global situation. At the same time, however, it is assumed that there are analytic units and processes that can underwrite thematizations and discourses that for the time being are adequate on empirical and epistemological grounds—that is, "make sense." Working within that framework, Robertson and Chirico propose that we think about globalization in terms of the interrelationships between four types of units (or systems or categories): selves, national societies, the world-system of societies, and the notion of humanity (or mankind). The fundamental feature of the globalization process according to Robertson and Chirico is the increasing relativization of units with respect to each other. In other words, globalization is the process whereby action by or within one unit is increasingly constrained by the necessity to take into account in some manner the actions or implications for action of other units on a worldwide basis.

The perspective proposed by Robertson and Chirico is formally closed in the sense that there is an implicit claim that the process of relativization is necessary and sufficient to account for the phenomenon of globalization. At the same time, the perspective is substantively open-ended and invites the analytic and empirical exploration of relations between units. Thus, for example, in explicating the self-and-world-system axis of the Robertson-Chirico framework in an earlier article, I have examined the notion of self-incorporation into the global system on the basis of psychodynamic repression and projection among those attracted to the New Christian Right in North America.[2] Here I will explore the question of whether there is any firm warrant for asserting that active, pragmatic self-definitions can occur vis-à-vis the properties of the emergent global system and how religion might enter into and affect such definitions.

EMPIRICAL BASES

The juxtaposition of two broad classes of empirical phenomena serves as a point of departure or "text" for developing an understanding of the nature of globalization, the self, and religion. The two classes of empirical phenomena are familiar enough. On the one hand, there are a host of things that underwrite the rubric "the world is getting smaller." The most central of these is the growth of population and its agglomeration in urban centers on a worldwide basis. To this must be added the increasing ease of global communication, transport, and travel that have accelerated the circulation of ideas, goods, and people so remarkably since the end of World War II.

While the emergence and growth of a biotechnological base (with essentially no degrees of freedom in the evolutionary process that are not traceable in some way to the action of *homo sapiens*) provide the infrastructure for globalization, the social sense that something is happening is traceable to the precipitation of organization in various institutional areas that have no boundaries on earth—except earth itself. Two examples suffice: Computer communications technology has brought about a global financial and currency market that never ceases operation. The deregulation of various stock markets—most notably the London market—is a direct response to the possibilities inherent in the global biotechnological revolution. The world's dominant powers—the Soviet Union and the United States—are in continuous active military and naval confrontation through technological means. The state of the art in that contest is found in the submarine "warfare" ongoing at this moment wherever there is ocean water.

The second set of empirical phenomena has to do with what could be called "The Fundamentalist Absolute in Postmodern Times" and encompasses, among other things, the rise to political prominence of absolutist trends and emphases within all of the so-called world religions.[3] These include, but are not limited to, the following familiar examples: Shi'a Islam in, particularly, its Iranian instantiation; the followers of Rabbi Meir Kahane in Israel and elsewhere; and the complex of individuals and organizations associated with the so-called New Christian Political Right in the United States. Less familiar examples can be found throughout Asia, Africa, Latin America, and Oceania. Only Antarctica and the territory above the Arctic Circle appear to be exempt from the carriers of an absolute religious doctrine with political implications.

These two classes of empirical phenomena constitute the material-organizational base of an increasingly small world and a collection of religious absolutes embodied in some way in societal organizational network configurations. What clues, if any, lay hidden in these empirical "haystacks" regarding emergent systemic social elements at the global level? Before attempting to answer that question I will impose two scope conditions that limit the range of answers. Both arise from a consideration of notions introduced above.

SCOPE CONDITIONS

First, the mention of the Soviet Union and the United States—the units of the bipolar superpower system—begs the question of a global "settlement" based on the ascendance of one or the other. It is very unlikely that a neoimperial model will prevail with either the Soviet Union or the United States securing the "upper hand" forever. That model implies either a centralized system of social-military control or a degree of identification of local interests with those of the center (or a mixture of both) that are unlikely. One requires a mobilization of force and a monitoring apparatus that, even if technically feasible, would be too costly in terms of developing concepts of human rights and the good life. The other assumes the willingness of "locals" to reinterpret and transform their interests in keeping with either a Great Russian or Anglo-American mold. If anything, recent history suggests that "locals" are increasingly resistant to reinterpretation of their interests in an incorporative, cosmopolitan direction. Palestinians, Punjabis, Tamils, Nicaraguans, and Afghans, among others, have all resisted incorporative efforts with violence. There is no reason to believe that incorporative efforts will not continue to be met by violence. From a political perspective, then, the contemporary state of the globe is characterized by interest definition at the nation-state level and the would-be-nation-state (or "persistent peoples") level and varying capacities to realize those interests in transnational interaction. The importance of that observation in the present context is that it suggests that the system of interaction between nations is not biased in a direction that would lead to the discovery of a common global purpose. If that were the case, we would be on familiar theoretical and empirical ground, but we are not.

The first scope condition, then, imposes the constraint of transnational interaction and relativization without the boundary of a common collective global purpose. The second limits the absoluteness of the so-called "fundamentalist absolute." Its essence is simply stated: fundamentalism as a generic category is modernism *in a formal sense*. From a formal point of view, the spirit of modernism entails breaking up a whole into abstracted component parts—the discovery (or construction) of the atom in modern physics, the "unnatural" abstractions of modern art, the promulgation of the Fundamentals of the Christian faith. There is no formal difference between, say, Duchamp's *Nude Descending a Staircase* and the list of the Fundamentals. Both are composed of abstracted components, with each component a simplified unit, that form a nonorganic whole. This "whole," thus, is a trick of the eye, a creation of faith, not reason.

Fundamentalisms are not atavistic social movements. Although fundamentalisms may be dialectical responses to modernization or modernism, the spirit of fundamentalism and the spirit of modernism are, essentially, the same. The deep structure of both is nonorganic abstraction. Far from being autonomous absolutes, fundamentalisms can be completely relativized through reduction to the form they share: modernism. Fundamentalisms, in other words, are a way of participating in modernity, or better yet, of "doing" modernity.[4]

If fundamentalisms are nonorganic abstraction, their relative prominence in the global system today can be a very important clue regarding the direction in which the system is going in terms of what might be called the formation and crystallization of action units. A major feature of nonorganic abstraction is the absence of the immanence of the object in its "representation." The immanence of an object can with effort be imposed by the eye in a cubist painting, but what is there to impose on the color-geometry of Ellsworth Kelly or Frank Stella except the immanence of abstraction itself? What is being "represented" in nonorganic abstraction, then, transcends the representation and may not be found in it. There is, in other words, something profoundly Protestant about nonorganic abstraction.[5] Where the form of Protestantism lurks, the modern self cannot be far behind.

Parenthetically, but not insignificantly, a case can also be argued that the "natural geometrics" of much Islamic art may represent an arrested modernistic tendency. Only a minimum amount of tampering would be required to convert it into nonorganic abstraction where representation of idealized forms becomes problematic. In a very broad sense, the possibilities for modern selfhood may be strongest in Islam compared with, for example, Hinduism or Buddhism.

GLOBAL SELFHOOD

But, it can be asked, is there any *firm* warrant for the claim, in terms of the properties of the emergent global system, that selfhood can be or is a feature of that system itself? These two scope conditions reveal two things. First, if the possibility for global selfhood exists, it cannot be by virtue of collective inclusion, since there is no global collectivity. Second, the visibility of fundamentalisms in the world arena suggests that we should look for properties that underwrite active, as contrasted to mystical, selfhood,[6] since nonorganic abstraction implies at the individual level an empowered, autonomous unit who stands over against and is defined by transcendent otherness.

What I am trying to do in the final analysis is determine whether it is even arguable that a basis exists for global selfhood that is biased in the direction of activity and mastery. In a very broad sense, I am exploring thematic elements that can be traced from Nietzsche (the hypersocial self), through Weber (the active, mastering self), to Parsons (the rationalization of the world through the diffusion of secularized Protestant forms and values) within a global frame of reference.

The Calvinist Model

Although the general form of the problematic with which we are dealing (namely, the self-society—or self-system—dialectic) is usually traced through German social thought, the dialectic was formulated by Calvin himself, when read within a Durkheimian framework (God symbolizing society). The first chapter of the *Institutes of the Christian Religion* is entitled "The Knowledge of God and That of Ourselves Are Connected. How They Are Interrelated," and the first two sentences read: "Nearly all the wisdom we possess, that is to say, true and sound wisdom, consists of two parts: the knowledge of God and of ourselves. *But, while joined by many bonds, which one precedes and brings forth the other is not easy to discern.*"[7]

Standing alone, Calvin's sentences pose in theological language the general sociological problematic of the self-system dialectic without suggesting how systemic variation underwrites different types of selves. It was, of course, Weber's point some 350 years later that the content of Calvin's theological system biased the self-society dialectic in the direction of the active self.

It is ironic that having explicated the emergence of the basis for the active, mastering self in Western culture, Weber was pessimistic about the social-organizational consequences of the action system surrounding and flowing from such selves. Increases in system rationalization place increasing constraints on the freedom of the self to maneuver in a field of action according to his analysis. This pessimism, however, can be read as typical Lutheran "inwardness" in which faith constructs an unassailable, quiescent, mystical, pietistic, romantic self that—come what may—cannot be conquered by the world and the devil (the "iron cage"). Like God, the self is a fortress, and the fortress is constructed by faith (alone). This theme finds its most notable expression in Thomas Luckmann's concept of privatized religion.[8]

If the organizational form of rationalization—bureaucracy—were globally expandable, the search for the basis of an active global self would be futile (assuming that the bureaucratic form does desiccate and squeeze the action field that contextualizes the active self).[9] Recently, however, some analysts have proposed that the bureaucratic model may not be infinitely expandable over extremely large domains of action.[10] This does not mean that organization cannot exist at the global level, but that its form is unlikely to resemble the structure of authority and the command and control networks that are embedded in administered bureaucratic systems. Markets, for example, *are* common at the global level and have been in some sense for centuries, as Wallerstein reminds us.[11] Markets, however, do not seem to possess the capacity to found selves, perhaps because the range of intention and gesture in a market is so limited.

(This may account in part for the tragic existence of pariah peoples who are encountered only in markets.)

If bureaucracy is, in fact, unable to organize the globe, this at least leaves open the question of the possibility of an active global self. It also underscores once again the weakness of conventional modes of socio-logical analysis as tools for grasping and constructing the global phenomenon. What does one do in the midst of what Raymond Aron, referring to the global situation, called "a-social society" and "anarchical order"—to which we might add "un-administered organization"?[12]

I think what might be called the "Calvinistic Reformed moment" in world history is paradigmatic. I refer not to the rise and spread of Genevan doctrine nor to its putative role in stimulating the capitalist form of economic organization. Rather, what I am referring to is the way in which Calvinism seemed to resonate with early nascent capitalism to underwrite the world-mastering, active self. What, it can be asked, were the systemic features of capitalism and Calvinism that were so in tune that out of their interpenetration came the active, mastering self? In other words, how did the interpenetration of the spirit of capitalism and inner-worldly asceticism configure a field of action that called forth the active self as a response?

In his recent exegesis of *The Protestant Ethic and the Spirit of Capitalism*, Gianfranco Poggi argues cogently that the central connection between the spirit of capitalism and inner-worldly asceticism is found in the parallel between the entrepreneur's exacting use of time in relentless systemic activity wherein every moment in the process of capital accumulation is treated as a potentially surplus-generating act and the Calvinist conception of calling in which the elect strives "to order reality in a dynamic, open-ended fashion, rather than accepting any given arrangement as final. . . . What is enjoined upon the Calvinist faithful by his anxious search for an assurance of salvation is the activity itself of ordering, rather than the acceptance of or the adaptation to any given pattern or order."[13] The ordering of "spiritual life" corresponds with the entrepreneur's action within an environment of competition, "which he must continuously monitor in order to meet the challenge presented by its objective developments. Thus, while a keen, calculating control over his own resources is at the heart of entrepreneurial activity, the latter is finalised to the external, objective test of competitiveness and profitability."[14]

Poggi's analysis turns on an interpretation of the interpenetration of two *moral* orders—the spirit of capitalism and Calvinistic inner-worldly asceticism. Without changing the inner logic of his argument regarding the correspondence between those moral orders, his exegesis of Weber can be usefully expanded in an analytic direction by posing two questions: First, what was the outcome or "dependent variable" in terms of the crystallization of action units? Second, what properties of the larger environment must be assumed to exist and call forth as a response the interpenetration of the two moral orders?

The answer to the first question has already been anticipated. The outcome of the interpenetration of the two moral orders is the active self. As regards the second question, it is at least plausible to assume that the moral orders and their interpenetration are contingent upon an environment that is continuous in time and provides by way of responsive feedback an objectified image of what is going on. Without continuity in time, there can be no systematically ordered activity. Without objectified feedback, there can be no evaluation of activity. These are the logically necessary analytic features of the environment to which the interpenetrating moral orders of the spirit of capitalism and Calvinistic inner-worldly asceticism were tuned and which, taken together, called forth the active self. The empirical milieu of Calvinism and early capitalism was characterized by the emergence of a "world" that as far as the field of action was concerned displayed the properties of continuity and feedback (or recursion). On this hypothesis we can ask: Do these properties characterize the emergent global situation today? It seems to me that they do, but before arguing that case briefly, it is important to clarify what is meant by continuity and recursion.

Continuity

Continuity means that there is a field of action such that an acting unit can act in it. A recognizable world is constituted, a world in which an acting unit can act over time. From the perspective of time, it is not necessary that this world be empirically existent on a moment-to-moment basis. Thus, the world of the preliterates that was the focus of Durkheim's analysis in *The Elementary Forms of the Religious Life* was characterized by continuity over time through gathering and dispersing and gathering again. What might be called "the pace of continuity," then, can vary. Obviously, the phenomenon of globalization involves an enormous increase in that pace—sometimes to the extent that an activity or structure exists without actually lapsing at any time—for example, the global money exchange market.

Recursion

Recursion is a term drawn from the language of mathematics and formal systems. One way of viewing recursion is that it involves what Hofstadter calls "strange loops," the property that no matter where one starts in a system and no matter how many transformed steps and nodes there are, one can return or get back to where one started or to a point that has already been traversed in the system. As Hofstadter points out, the drawings of the Dutch artist Escher and the music of J. S. Bach exemplify recursion.[15]

Regarding emergent globalization, recursion entails an enhancement of the likelihood that the effects of an acting unit's acts will traverse a system that is bounded by nothing except the earth itself, and will return to the acting unit in an objectified form that can be evaluated. Sociologists are most familiar with recursion in terms of the self-other dialectic that forms the basis of G. H. Mead's analysis.[16] Globalization involves an expansion of that dialectic both in terms of the number and location of possible others and the number of nodes or networks through which the effects of self's action travel before coming "home."

Recursion and continuity are necessary properties of a field of action in which the active self can emerge. They are not, however, both necessary and sufficient for emergence to occur. The "software" of meaning and hermeneutic certainly must be added to the "hardware" of global continuity and recursion before the system will "boot" a self. For example, with reference to the paradigmatic case of Calvinism, Poggi notes that the Calvinistic Protestant was a "tensed up" person, self-mobilizing and active. That penchant for action sprang from the inner "psycho-logic" of Calvinism as a system of doctrine and ethics. In other words, Calvinism mobilized individuals for action within an inner-worldly ascetic moral-ethical frame of reference that was in correspondence with the capitalist "spirit" (or moral-ethical frame of reference), both being responsive to a larger milieu characterized by continuity and recursion.

The Contemporary Situation

As regards religious input into the contemporary global situation, it may be the case that radical forms of religious absolutism, including Christian Fundamentalism, have a peculiar advantage over more relativized forms of faith and practice when it comes to self-formation vis-à-vis the emergent global situation. As Stark and Bainbridge have pointed out, the compensators associated with religious absolutisms have formidable sense-making powers at the individual level.[17] Thus, religious absolutisms enter the circuitry of the global situation as over-capitalized modules of individualized meaning well able to withstand the inevitable reductions in the power to confer meaning that can accompany the processes of relativization that, according to Robertson and Chirico, constitute globalization. This being the case, the field of action defined by continuity and recursion at the global level may be peculiarly vulnerable to self-formation congealed around religious absolutes. The empirical prominence of religious absolutes in the contemporary global situation would seem to sustain this conclusion, at least for the moment.

More generally, any identity packages that are densely self-reflexive and have degrees of freedom that are not firmly context-bound (a characteristic of normative systems that are well internalized at the individual level) or are supported by a tightly circumscribed local group with an effective economy of symbols, would seem to be candidates for survival and expansion in the diffuse global network of action possibilities. Such packages have the capacity to be read into the global circuitry without dilution of meaning. They have great staying power because they are firmly rooted in individual or local systems that are well defended against the debilitating effects of relativization.

Among all the modes of cultural expression that humankind has produced in its evolutionary history, identity packages that are densely self-reflexive and relatively context-free seem to have been spun out more often than not by religion. In considering the contemporary global situation, then, there is good reason to pay attention to the nature of religious movements and currents at the global level, not because religion has or should have any cognitively or epistemologically privileged position in the examination of the emergent situation, but because religion in its various forms may be one product of the evolution of the human species that contains elements that have the capacity to sustain meaningful action in the global context at the individual level.

4

Globalism and Inclusion: Theoretical Remarks on the Non-Solidary Society

Peter F. Beyer

It is not difficult today to argue that for a great many people the social world has become coextensive with the globe. The proliferation of mass media of communication, worldwide trade, tourism, quick means of transportation, long-range military technologies, and the like have made it seem to many that what happens on Vanuatu or Sakhalin Island may be as important for people in Toronto or "Middletown" to know as what happens locally or nationally. In one of its prime aspects, this globality is constituted temporally: events in faraway places are a matter for communication to worldwide locales very quickly. This rapidity makes possible the truly social dimension of globality: what people do in one place on the globe may well be done in the direct context of what other people are doing twenty thousand miles away. The expectations that structure our actions here can and do include expectations of the actions of people in very diverse and distant places; and this expectation structure is reciprocal. What some people do in British Columbia may have everything to do with what is done and expected of them in the Punjab. A problem in a factory in Bangkok may lead me to change my plans for the weekend, if I had intended to visit the person who is called upon to solve them.

On one level, the central problem of this globality can be described simply as a clash of cultures. Previously relatively isolated societies are now in more or less constant contact with one another, leading to the kinds of conflict one might expect when differing views of the world are at stake. In recent social-scientific discussion on globalism, however, this view has been incorporated as only one aspect of a much more general problem centering on how global order is itself to be conceived.[1] In this context, clash of cultures as a description is oversimplified: it does not tell us enough about what is clashing. It is my contention in this chapter that to conceive what global order is, and therefore to assess its problems adequately, we must have a more precise idea of the difference between what the order was *before* it became global and what it is or is becoming *now*.

In what follows, I will suggest the outlines of a theoretical approach to the problem of globalism on the basis of selected aspects of the general theory of social systems and society of Niklas Luhmann. My purpose is not simply to exegete what Luhmann himself has said in his own publications but rather to explore its possibilities for conceiving the global social order and compare them in a preliminary way with other efforts in this direction. Specifically, I begin by outlining how, in the Luhmannian scheme of things, the global system must be conceived sociologically in the first order as a single global society. This is followed by a consideration of the possible reasons why relatively few other contributions to the discussion on globality have heretofore felt it warranted to speak about the global system as a society and speak instead about societies that are in one sense or another part of this global whole. Next, I discuss the consequences of the Luhmannian view for the relation between the individual and modern society under the headings of inclusion and exclusivity. The analysis of inclusion leads into a consideration of what place personal identity and collective solidarity have in the model thus presented. Finally, in the context of contemporary politicized religious movements, I explore some possible relations between these movements, the religious system of modern society, and the problems of globality.

GLOBAL SYSTEM AS GLOBAL SOCIETY

The Luhmannian perspective sees society as the encompassing social system of all acts communicatively accessible to one another on the basis of meaning.[2] The precise derivation of this definition need not concern us here; its implications for the problem under discussion do. Starting from this conception, for there to be more than one society, there must be a sufficient degree of communicative discontinuity between groups of actors to make the opportunities for communication rare and restricted. Practically, this means both consistent physical separation and relatively little overlap in the meaning of acts. The definition almost forces the conceiving of the contemporary global social system as a society.[3] Besides contradicting alternative ideas of what constitutes a society (a topic discussed below), it shifts the theoretical problem away from how fundamentally similar yet disparate parts can possibly come to form a whole to how the parts have changed in terms of which the whole is constituted. Put more in terms of sociological theory, it shifts the problem from one of *integration* to one of *differentiation*.[4]

From the Luhmannian point of view, modern society is a consequence of a change in Western society in the type of inner-societal differentiation that dominates. Unlike, for instance, Spencer, Durkheim, or Parsons, Luhmann sees modernity as being characterized not primarily by a quantitative increase in differentiation, but more important, by a qualitative change in the criterion according to which primary societal subsystems are formed.[5] To conceive the characteristic differentiation of modern society, it is not enough to look to an increase in the division of labor (e.g., Durkheim), an increase in the differentiation of functional subsystems (e.g., Parsons), and/or a shift in dominance of one subsystem over others (e.g., Spencer). These features are not denied as such, but they are seen as not getting at the most crucial aspect of the change, which is a shift from a dominance of *stratified* differentiation to a dominance of *functional* differentiation.[6]

All the various ramifications of this different conceptualization cannot, of course, be presented here. Certain salient features, however, must be extracted to see what the implications are for conceiving modern global society. First, there is the principle that stratification can be a form of subsystem differentiation and not just the unequal distribution of status, wealth, power, and the like.[7] Stratificatory differentiation forms subsystems on the basis of rank: to which stratum or class does an action belong? The presence and importance of functional distinctions—such as the division of labor or specialized institutions like bureaucracies and churches—are not denied for stratified societies; but they are seen as woven as much as possible into the stratified structures, providing aspects of the context in which they operate. By contrast, modern society forms its principal subsystems on the basis of function, that is, on the basis of what fundamental problem is addressed. Instead of, for instance, nobilities, merchant, and peasant strata (systems), one now deals with political, economic, and religious systems. Again, stratification is not thereby excluded from modern society, but it now no longer operates as the structuring principle of the primary societal subsystems.

The sociostructural shift from stratification to function can be further understood in terms of fundamental principles of order or selection. Here we are looking at a key ideological correlate of the change, one that will be reflected in the conception that the respective societies have of themselves and also, therefore, the conception that observers can have of them. Luhmann describes this change as one from *hierarchy* to *function*.[8] Implied in the idea of function is a comparison of functional equivalents: if function is the relation of a structure or process to a particular problem, then the problem provides the perspective from which to compare alternative solutions.[9] Contained in the Luhmannian notion of function, therefore, is a fundamental relativization and hence equality of that which fulfills functions. To bring the discussion back to the shift from the hierarchical to the functional ordering principle, one can formulate the difference in terms of Louis Dumont's analysis of value: whereas premodern, stratified societies generated the fundamental value of hierarchical *order*, modern functionally differentiated society generates the fundamental value of functional *choice*.[10]

The connection between the shift from stratified to functional differentiation and that from territorial to global societies can, from this Luhmannian perspective, be understood in terms of the conditions for the possibility of conceiving society as territorial. Stratified societies put a limit on how complex they can get because they depend for their reproduction on the concentration of most societal communicative resources in the hands of a quite small upper class. The limitation of collective action to that which can be controlled by the action of a tiny minority sets limits to the spatial (and temporal) extension of the society as a whole, albeit quite imprecise ones.[11] In such a situation, it makes sense to conceive society as territorially based, particularly when the base of power and wealth of the aristocracies is land or specific location. The structural limitations are therefore reflected and reinforced in the self-conception of such societies.[12]

With modern society, the change to functionally differentiated structures eliminates the possibility of territorial limitation of the society as a whole. Each of the principal subsystems, whether economic, political, scientific, religious, or other has its own, relatively independent structural perspective on the society as a whole: the range of economic activity, for instance, cannot be consistently integrated with political criteria; so with the relation of all the subsystems. The relations among the systems are nonhierarchical, making it difficult to order or conceive the society as a whole in terms of the selection criteria of any one of the subsystems as in stratified societies. Only the political system still relies heavily on territorial divisions, but even here, the arbitrary (i.e., based on choice that visibly could have transpired otherwise), and yet for *political* reasons, stable nature of these divisions is recognized.[13] The economic system, by contrast, runs so counter to territoriality, that it has hitherto provided one of the most productive perspectives for conceiving globality as a system.[14] Similarly, the scientific, familial, health, artistic-cultural, religious, and even educational systems all defy territorialization to a large degree, or at least cannot all be integrated within a single set of territorial divisions.

In the Luhmannian scheme of things, it is the differentiation of modern society itself that is at the source of difficulties in conceiving global society or even a global system in a univocal way. The characteristic problems and crises of this global system are therefore also to be understood in terms of this fundamental structural feature and its consequences. However, Luhmann's ideas on the subject are, to say the least, not widely shared by other scholars concerned with the question of globalism. Much of this divergence is attributable to the dominance in the discussion of a conception of society that makes it difficult to see the global system as a social system, let alone a global society.[15] It is to a comparison of the Luhmannian model with this more dominant one that I now turn.

SOCIETIES AND INTEGRATION

The current discussion of globalism does not generally use the term territorial society, but rather favors expressions like "national societies," when the term "society" is qualified at all.[16] Most often, the literature seems to assume that, whatever a society is, when referring to the global level, one must speak in the plural: societies. That the term therefore has a territorial reference appears obvious. What is less obvious, but what is clearly brought out in the Luhmannian perspective, is that it also has a political, perhaps more precisely, a politico-moral, reference. Saying "national societies" expresses this nicely without having simply to identify society with state, something that would be too easy to call into question. It also indicates that society and culture are somehow coterminous. While the insistence on a plurality of societies in the current global context points to the undeniable multiplicity of important regional, cultural, political, ethnic, and religious differences, the impossibility of drawing a single set of boundaries that encompasses all of these important differences in a consistent and convincing way without reducing them to one of their number leads one to look at how societies are explicitly or implicitly conceived so that this fuzziness of the concept results. In this regard, the equally vague idea of *integration* plays a key role.

The notion that social order must somehow be positively reinforced by specific social structures that guarantee the order without the constant threat and application of physical force goes back at least to Aristotle in the Western tradition. In modern sociology, the best-known example of the persistence of this tradition is to be found in Durkheim's claim, formulated in reaction to the utilitarians, that, beyond contract, there are normative structures, particularly common beliefs, that operate to guarantee the highly differentiated whole.[17]

Given the Luhmannian theoretical perspective, undoubtedly the most interesting exemplification of this tradition is Talcott Parsons's general theory of action. Here society, as the I-subsystem of the general system of action, is principally dedicated to the function of integration. At the core of the societal system itself is the societal community whose primary function is again integration. Its structural component is norms.[18] Societies depend on the establishment and maintenance of the loyalty of the members to the societal community and hence are structures dependent on feelings of solidarity. From this angle, conceiving the global system as a society becomes virtually a contradiction in terms under current historical conditions.

From the Luhmannian perspective, such a conception of society is too much rooted in historical stratified structures in which whole individuals were much more closely identified with particular subsystems of society and to the critical importance of kinship groups and residential communities in these structures. As such, it is inadequate for conceiving the modern situation where functional differentiation and global communication dominate. This returns us to what was discussed earlier as a shift, in Luhmannian theory, from integration to differentiation. Conceiving the fundamental global problem in terms of integration is reflected in an emphasis on problems of solidarity, community, identity, or with Robertson, for instance, telic ends that set the larger context in terms of which the global system can be identified.[19] Luhmann describes such problems as being ones of the difficulty modern society has in coming up with consistent self-descriptions or self-conceptions. Identity refers to the relation of the system to itself. It is not what constitutes the system as system.[20]

This brings us to the central point of difference. Luhmann's conception of society is different because his idea of what constitutes a system is different. For Luhmann, a system, including a social system, including society, constitutes itself by establishing a *difference* between the system and its environment. The system is not what it is by virtue of the internal ordering of its elements (in the case of social systems, actions), but by the *continuous* and *recursive* reproduction of those elements in a way that constitutes a difference between the system and its environment. This difference or differentiation in itself already guarantees the identity or integration of the system. Additional arrangements that focus on identity can then be seen as addressing a wide variety of nevertheless important problems; but they are not constitutive of the system itself. Societies, therefore, in contradiction to Durkheim, are not distinguished as to type by different ways of integration (mechanical or organic solidarity), but rather by different forms of differentiation.

While these highly abstract formulations may be of interest to those concerned with general theory in sociology, they have been introduced here because of the implications for how we are to regard and what we can expect from the contemporary global system. It is to some of these implications that I now turn.

INCLUSION AND EXCLUSIVITY

Shifting one's theoretical view from integration to differentiation allows the former to be conceived negatively: problems of integration now refer to difficulties in reproducing differentiation. To take but one example, the relations of church and state, or more broadly, the relations of the religious and political subsystems of modern society, are today often characterized by conflict and even crisis.[21] From Latin America to the Philippines, from Egypt to the United States, the examples are varied and consistent, in spite of fluctuations in scholarly and media attention. From the Luhmannian perspective, the *global* integrative problem reflected in these conflicts is not to be addressed in terms of how the religious and politicial selectivities or interests are to be reconciled, but rather in terms of how the interference between the two systems can be kept at a level that still allows each its relative autonomy to function properly. The issue is not to harmonize the two systemic perspectives into a hierarchical order but to maintain the differentiation. Tension and conflict are therefore endemic to functionally differentiated systems, and the problem of integration thus appears as a problem of not negating the differentiation.[22] On the semantic level, the new situation of modern society is reflected in the emphasis on detente rather than victory, plurality rather than unification, tolerance rather than imposition, justice as equality rather than justice as order.

The shift from integration to differentiation is also manifested in the Luhmannian conception of inclusion. Again, rather than being the positive term referring to integrative processes in response to evolutionary change that it is with Parsons, it becomes a negatively conceived term referring to the elimination of structures that negate functional differentiation.[23] This shift requires some explanation, not least because of its implications for thinking about the nature of the individual in modern society.

In Luhmann's theory, social systems are conceived in such a way that the psychic systems of individual human beings are not part of the social system. Society does not consist of human beings but of their actions. The detailed reasons for this mutual exclusivity need not concern us here. Suffice it to say that Luhmann analyzes the difference in terms of a distinction between consciousness and communication and the self-referential or autopoeic character of systems in general.[24]

The universal tendency to think of society as composed of human beings is then traced to the structural features of premodern societies. Thus, for example, in a stratified society virtually all the actions of an individual human being are attributed to one principal subsystem of that society, his or her class. It therefore makes sense to conceive the relation of the individual to society as one of a part belonging to the whole. With the shift to functional differentiation, this kind of wholesale allocation becomes very difficult: if many of my actions are elements in the scientific subsystem of society, many also are not. I act in my family, in the economy, in the polity, and so on. Since the problem of integration is one of maintaining differentiation, the response of inclusion must be seen in this light. To avoid excessive interference of the subsystems with each other, a functionally differentiated society will have a tendency to abstract the actions that compose its subsystems from the individuals to which these actions are also attributed. Modern society will therefore tend to be highly impersonal in most of its systems but will also not exclude a person from participation in one system on the basis of personal attributes that belong to another system or are simply not functionally relevant. This negative inclusion is exemplified in politico-legal bills of rights that forbid discrimination on the basis of various personal attributes but say little about what *should be* the basis of discrimination. It is assumed that discrimination will take place on the basis of "merit," that is, according to the selection criteria of the system involved, not those that might operate in that system's environment.[25] Thus, access to health care should not be influenced by economic status, but rather by medical need; admission and advancement in the educational system should not be influenced by family criteria (e.g., race, sex), but by educational merit, and so forth. For the society as a whole, the fact of discrimination is not in itself seen to be a problem, but rather a necessity. What is perceived to be a problem is the fact that such discrimination still very often happens on a basis other than function.[26]

Luhmann's negative formulation of the concept of inclusion has significant implications for the place of the individual in modern society. If all the actions of an individual can no longer be seen very easily as part of one subsystem as contrasted to others, then individuals will appear in much sharper profile to their social environment. The increased societal complexity that accompanies the shift to functional differentiation also increases the variety of life circumstances in which individuals can find themselves.[27] As a result, modern society is characterized by the much discussed increase in the individualization of individuals. To the phenomenon of inclusion corresponds a great increase in the exclusivity of individual psychic systems. Without the necessity of coordinating his or her selectivity with one dominant subsystem of society, the individual is left "free" to develop in a larger variety of directions. Indeed, functional specialization as the dominant mode of subsystem formation requires this variety. Inclusion of all individuals in all subsystems is therefore accompanied by greater mutual exclusivity of the same individuals. This will seem to be a paradox only if inclusion is conceived as positive incorporation in a societal community that in some sense represents the society as a whole.

Increased individualization and the individualism that is its ideological correlate bring with them problems of personal identity and the relation of the individual to society. From the Luhmannian perspective, the latter is characterized by greater independence and greater interdependence at the same time.[28] In certain of its aspects, this combination is evident in the simultaneity of exclusivity and inclusion. The former, personal identity, is to be defined as the relation of the psychic system to itself. As such it involves the realm of what Luhmann discusses under the heading of self-descriptions and self-observations.[29] It is here that questions that in most of the literature on these topics appear as problems of integration surface. It is therefore to these that we must turn for an understanding of the Luhmannian perspective on problems of identity and, by extension, solidarity in the context of modern global society.

SELF-DESCRIPTION, IDENTITY, AND SOLIDARITY

Far from being minor matters in his theory, self-descriptions have an important place in the Luhmannian scheme of things. They operate within a system to represent the system as a whole in distinction from its environment. They are, however, to be distinguished from self-observation, which refers to the fact that systems must be able to control what is to be treated as system and what as environment. Self-observation is an aspect of what allows the system to reproduce itself as system/environment distinction. Self-description is the thematization of that observation.[30]

Self-description therefore is closely related to the identity of a system, that is, its relation to itself. Self-description reproduces the system/environment distinction within the system for the sake of greater control over the system's selectivity. This becomes especially important when the complexity of the environment increases, thus forcing the system either to increase its complexity (or, what amounts to the same, its selectivity) or take the risk of ignoring what is happening in the environment.

These abstract formulations can be concretized somewhat by looking at the situation of the individual in modern society discussed above. The heightened exclusivity of personal identity is reflected in the fact that the range of possibilities for how each personal system is to be constituted increases greatly. The individual person, as psychic system, now must select from a greater number of possibilities, and this in interpenetration with his or her social environment as well as with the relative certainty that other persons, perhaps most others, will select in a different way. The selection criteria for this personal determination are not given in any sort of complete way by society itself which, as functionally differentiated, tends only to help determine certain of his or her actions from any one point of reference. In addition, the functional subsystems themselves, because they are not hierarchically ordered, may indicate determinations in contradictory directions. The result is a problem of identity for the individual that must be solved through consistent self-description. Accordingly, identifications may proceed along highly idiosyncratic lines. They may concentrate on one subsystem as opposed to others—a person may identify herself with a career or as a family member or as a member of a political unit, an economic class, or as a religious believer—or may combine specifications from a number of sources in a way that lets self-description vary according to situation and/or crisis. The contexts in which personal self-descriptions are formed is therefore characterized by variety and change, something that is only chaos or anomie if the self-description bases itself on unchanging order rather than situational choice.[31]

If the problems of personal identity can thus be treated as ones of self-description at the level of the individual, problems of self-description at the level of social systems can be treated under the heading of solidarities. To approach this topic properly from a Luhmannian perspective requires a preliminary examination of types of social systems. Here Luhmann distinguishes interaction, organizational, and societal systems. Briefly, interaction systems are characterized by face-to-face communication among persons present; organizational systems are based on the distinction between members and nonmembers, as well as the rules that distinguish between the two; and societal systems are the encompassing systems in which the other two operate.[32]

For the current discussion, perhaps the most important aspect of this typology is that, as societies become more complex (and modern, functionally differentiated society is much more complex than previous stratified societies), these three types of social systems both proliferate and become more differentiated from each other. There are more and a greater variety of interactions, organizations, and societal systems, but societal systems become less and less organizational, while organizations and societal systems reach levels of complexity where they can be conceived less and less as consisting of interactions. Accordingly, in the modern context, analyses that concentrate on one type of system cannot easily be transferred to the others.

One critical example can suffice here to illustrate this point. Society, in the modern context, is not an organization in the Luhmannian sense of the term. There are, first, no consistent rules of membership. Political citizenship crosses with cultural or ethnic belonging, and neither nor both of these can be automatically integrated with religious adherence. Family membership, while being a reason why most states grant uniform citizenship, crosses ethnic and/or religious boundaries. Unless society is identified simply with the political subsystem of society (i.e., the state), applying membership criteria to this level of social system can lead only to confusion. Moreover, an emphasis on political criteria leaves unanswered the question of why other criteria, such as economic, religious, and cultural ones, should not take precedence.

If it is argued, on the other hand, that this conflict of memberships in the modern context is precisely responded to by a general univer-salistic membership, as in the Parsonian conception of inclusion, then it must be asked what the criteria of such inclusive membership are, if they are not global. Again, establishing precedence or, what is the same, integrating various criteria of membership under one heading, be it political, ethnic, religious, or (especially) moral, becomes difficult if not impossible under modern conditions: the Islamic *umma* crosses state boundaries, many people in Canada consider the citizenship they have in common with other Canadians to be accidental if not simply unjust, and it is becoming increasingly difficult to assume that large multina-tional corporations have their prime loyalty to the country of their head offices.

If the idea of membership in a society that is not global creates diffi-culties in the modern social world, withdrawal of membership, or ex-clusion, does so as well and for the same reasons: unless society is arbitrarily defined as coincident with political or other criteria, the dif-ferent rules for exclusion that apply to different categories cannot be integrated.

The argument presented here does not contradict the validity of ana-lyzing various social collectivities in terms of membership/nonmember-ship and the rules attached to these. The point is rather that such analyses cannot be used to tell us what society *is* in the modern situation, because there is no consistent way of establishing an *order* among them according to hierarchy: they remain *choices* according to functions.

The upshot of this discussion is that, from the Luhmannian perspec-tive, solidarities on the level of society as a whole cannot be analyzed adequately with categories applicable primarily to organizations. Rather, the problem of solidarity must be seen as a problem of self-description in abstraction from the type of system under discussion. Again, seeing solidarity as a matter of self-description, rather than as immediately constitutive of social systems as such, is not to say that solidarity or the identity of collectivities is not of vital importance to this theoretical po-sition—quite the contrary. Because Luhmann can see only one society in the current global situation, the problem of self-description comes into sharp profile as characteristic of that society.

As mentioned above, the functional differentiation of modern society creates a society in which no one part is easily conceived to stand for the whole. To be sure, the dominance of one subsystem over shorter or longer periods and in different geographical regions may make it ap-propriate to conceive of this society as characterized by the typical se-lection criteria of that subsystem. Thus, it made some sense in the nineteenth century to describe that society (at least in the West) as bourgeois capitalist, reflecting a dominance of the economic subsystem. Similarly, it may make some sense today to think of the global order as primarily political, although as just outlined, this is not without certain difficulties.[33] Similarly, the all-pervasiveness of techno-scientific applications to the various problems faced by our society may make it tempting to define our society in terms of scientific achievements, while certain Middle Eastern perspectives may justifiably define global reality primarily in religious terms. All of these possibilities—and others—are alternatives, but none of them can impose itself as the obvious solution to the problem of *global* society's self-description.

Since, on the Luhmannian model, questions of solidarity are in the first order questions of self-description, our global society is to be characterized by its lack of solidarity. We live in a non-solidary society that nevertheless produces a tremendous variety of often exclusive subsolidarities, any of which could take situational and temporary precedence depending on whom one asks. Global order as global society therefore contains within itself the seeds of constant crisis and conflict: crisis as different problems generated in different subsystems become acute, and conflict as the competition between different perspectives and identities manifests itself. To be sure, the basic problem of self-description in modern global society remains a problem, and those who claim that the Luhmannian view offers no solid way of searching for the bases of global solidarity are undoubtedly correct. The critical question, however, is not whether Luhmann offers such a possibility. Rather, it is one of prognosis: Is the continued development of global order possible without such solidarity? Or, to put it expressly into Luhmannian terms: Does the level of societal complexity generated by a dominance of functional differentiation defy the self-description of the global societal system, and if so, does this mean the reterritorialization into societies and/or the redifferentiation of society?[34]

I cannot answer this question here. Suffice it to say that those contributors to the discussion of global reality who, implicitly or explicitly, are seeking answers to this question or attempting to find the seeds of such solidarity are not, from the Luhmannian point of view, addressing an illusory problem or even one of secondary importance.[35] This is not the point. What is the point is that, using the Luhmannian perspective, the question does not have an obvious answer, since the problem is not rooted in the insufficient sociality of global reality, but rather in the structural characteristics of a social reality that has been able to "go global."

RELIGION AND GLOBALISM

At the end of an article entitled, "The World Society as a Social System," Luhmann, in referring precisely to the problem just outlined, writes, "It may remain unsuccessful, but I cannot find it ridiculous."[36]

The implicit faith statement contained here points to a dimension of the question that, in terms of functionalist sociology (not to mention theology), is a religious one. The central position in stratified societies of a religio-cosmic vision and its concomitant structures in the integration of the divergent moral perspectives of the different strata indicates that religion has, in the past, served (among other things) in the capacity of "source of societal self-description." It is conceivable that it may again do this for global society today, perhaps through an "ecumenical theology" in the style of Wilfred Cantwell Smith or Hans Küng, perhaps through some as yet embryonic form of global civil religion based on human rights and cultural diversity.[37]

From the Luhmannian perspective, however, doubts begin to creep in as soon as one takes into consideration that the religious system of global society is not exempt from the consequences of the nonhierarchical relation among subsystems. Even if it is acknowledged that the religious function is located at such a basic level of social reality that it can be seen as addressing the whole of society more than other subsystems, the whole, under modern conditions, does not take priority over the parts, since each encompasses the world through its own system/environment relation. A self-description based on religion may condition the inner-societal environment of the political system and thereby render a political solution to a political crisis more likely. But it cannot be part of a religious resolution to a political crisis. The common parenthood of God cannot bridge the conflicting political claims of Israelis and Palestinians, even though interreligious dialogue may make the process easier. Appeals to social justice will not solve the crisis in the world banking system, although the protestations of churchmen may help prepare Western investors to accept some losses. It is in interpenetration with the other subsystems of global society that religion can contribute to its own development and to the development of the other subsystems, and it is through performance outputs that the religious systems can contribute to the solution of problems generated in other systems. But these possibilities point to anything but the kind of uniform self-description of a global social order expressive of an inclusive core solidarity.

This is, of course, not to deny the societal self-descriptive potential of religion. But given the fact that the strong religious traditions of today for the most part have *not* abandoned a form of expression that correlates more with stratified, territorial societies than with the conflictual, choice-oriented society of today—and given that religious institutions today seem more inclined to "take sides" and hence manifest structural conflicts more than seek to harmonize them—it is probably more likely that religion today will also be found more often helping to define major subsolidarities, and if anything, attempting to globalize them.

Politicized religious movements (or perhaps religiously inspired political movements) such as those in the Islamic world, the religious right
in the United States, Judaic orthodoxy in Israel, Sikh nationalism in the
Punjab, liberation theology movements in Latin America, the Caribbean,
South Africa, and elsewhere, Soka Gakkai in Japan, and others, all have
a limited territorial base that serves as their dominant focus. This fact
is commensurate with the segmental and territorial differentiation that
prevails in the modern global political system. To be sure, many such
movements, especially Christian liberation theologies and Islamic ones,
do situate themselves more or less in the global context. This feature,
however, is more reflective of the disparities between political and religious (and often ethnic) systemic boundaries than it is indicative of the
development of a global orientation as such. The religious system itself
is also a global system. It can generate a global perspective, a conception
of global reality that is fundamentally religious.[38] What it cannot do very
easily is coordinate or integrate that perspective (from whatever religious
tradition or combination of traditions it may be formulated) with all the
different, yet nevertheless also global, perspectives of the other systems,
especially the political, the economic, and the scientific.

The problem of global solidarity is also not located only in the plurality
of nonhierarchically ordered societal subsystems. In addition to the pluralism of function, there is the potentially much more varied pluralism
that is reflected in the exclusivity of individual psychic systems. The
potential that these have for forming solidary groups is not exhausted
by the division of society into functional subsystems, or even by the
internal differentiation of these systems (e.g., economic classes, religious
traditions, cultural ethnoses, families, business organizations, political
parties, states, unions). The seemingly inexhaustible variety of such
groupings makes it seem unlikely that a type of solidarity can be formed
on the global level that will take precedence over whatever is from time
to time locally more engaging.[39]

SUMMARY AND CONCLUSION

The thrust of this chapter has been to present a Luhmannian perspective on the theoretical problem of global social order. This theoretical
position conceives society in such a way that modern reality can be
characterized as one in which there is only one society, which is global
in extent. This globality is the result of a fundamental shift in the way
societies form their primary subsystems. Specifically, traditional societies
were differentiated into subsystems primarily according to strata and
hierarchically ordered according to rank. Modern society, by contrast,
has switched to functional determination of its primary subsystems, with
the result that the territorial reference of the more traditional societies

can no longer be maintained. This leads to an expansion of "society" to encompass all human communication around the globe. This theoretical position corresponds to a shift in conceiving social and global order from one seeing the primary sociological problem as one of integration to one seeing it as one of differentiation. The theory therefore sees itself as an aspect of the object that it is observing and describing, since to the shift from stratified to functional differentiation corresponds a shift from a primacy of integration to one of differentiation. Among the many consequences of this shift is the reformulation of key concepts, including that of society itself. Other critical concepts such as inclusion, identity, and solidarity are also objects of this reformulation, leading to a negative notion of inclusion, with identity and solidarity as terms referring to the problem of the self-description of systems.

Perhaps the key conclusion to be drawn from this neofunctional perspective is that the modern global order is not only a society, but is also characterized by a functional and personal pluralism that makes it very difficult, if not impossible, to arrive at a generally communicable self-description of that society and therefore at a global solidarity. The world order as we currently have it is one in which crisis and conflict are structurally endemic. As such, the Luhmannian position is different in its formulation of the problem, but perhaps not that different in material result. What makes the Luhmannian perspective valuable in the context of conceiving global order is that it offers a way of discerning the "larger but less obvious unities in social reality" without confusing this task with the much more difficult assignment of institutionalizing a global societal self-description.[40]

Finally, the perspective presented here casts doubt on attempts to look to religion for a solution to the basic problem of global society— and therefore one attempts to see a development in this direction in the various religious movements that have achieved such a high profile in the contemporary world (especially those with strong political manifestations). Rather than providing a solution to the problem, religion can perhaps best be asked to continue furnishing the faith that it may yet be solved, one way or another, before our exclusivities exclude us all.

5

Ultimate Values in Politics:
Problems and Prospects for
World Society

William H. Swatos, Jr.

In his seminal essay "Politics as a Vocation," Max Weber argued that
ultimate values have no place in politics in modern, rational-legal societies; political decisions are best made, he claimed, on instrumental
considerations. Religious commitments, furthermore, are particularly
pernicious elements to effective decision making. Likewise, in a recent
work, *Reactionary Modernism: Technology, Culture, and Politics in Weimar
and the Third Reich*, Jeffrey Herf has argued that it was precisely the
inclusion of ultimate values in the politics of a technological society that
characterized Nazi Germany as a unique system of political oppression.
The period following World War II, thus, was one in which "good
politics" was considered a politics free from ideology—an attitude epit-
omized in Daniel Bell's work *The End of Ideology*. Though Westerners of
course would resist the assertions of the Eastern bloc, Marxists also claim
that their politics is nonideological.
    In practice, however, ultimate values continued to be articulated in
politics, but at a global, rather than national, level. "Human rights" and
"the rights of the people," clearly ultimate values, came to replace particularistic slogans in value discourse. As conceptualized by the charter
and operation of the United Nations, for example, this most frequently meant the rights of nation-states.[1] Relatively little was done to
ensure human rights for individuals on an intranational basis by world-
societal organizations (until this gap was recognized and specific organizations developed to address it—e.g., Amnesty International). Nation-
state self-determination (i.e., political independence) was often considered the objective evidence of an expression of "the will of the people,"
hence human rights. Frank Lechner has termed this condition "insti-

tutionalized societalism"—a global phenomenon to be compared and contrasted to Talcott Parsons's "institutionalized individualism," itself critical to the development of Western democratic nation-states at an earlier historical period.

The resurgence of religious concerns in politics during the 1970s (and continuing into the present) throughout the world has been widely observed in both popular and scholarly literature. Most frequently emphasized in this discussion have been "fundamentalist" movements— notably in some Islamic nations and in the United States. Action on the political-religious right, however, does not exhaust the introduction of religiously based ultimate value systems into the political arena. Liberation theology in Latin America is evidence of a similar resurgence of explicitly religious ultimate values into political activity, as Roland Robertson, for example, has noted.[2] The issue of religion-and-politics, then, far from differentiating liberation theology from Islamic fundamentalism, identifies similarities between them; the relative universalism or particularism, respectively, of their discourses of ultimate values is what sets them apart. Liberation theology thus claims to assert "basic human rights," whereas Islamic fundamentalism asserts Islamic rights. Fundamentalist movements—Islamic, Zionist, Christian, or whatever—appear potentially threatening to the positive valences associated with the concept of a "world society," because of their value particularism. A similar illustrative case can be made for differing associations of leftist and rightist movements with respect to, say, "religious liberty," "self-determination," and other ultimate value orientations.

In their seminal essay, "Humanity, Globalization, and Worldwide Religious Resurgence," Robertson and Chirico compare and contrast a dualistic cosmology of individual-society relationships with a more holistic, global sense of humanity-world concerns. This chapter is intended to extend their model to the problem-context of the relationship of universalistic and particularistic invocations of ultimate values in the contemporary political arena. Continuing Robertson and Chirico's line of argument, along with that of Lechner in this volume, I suggest that in modernity at the nation-state level, much the same crisis is taking place in institutionalized societalism as that which characterized institutionalized individualism prior to the emergence of the modern welfare state. At the core of institutionalized individualism is the one-man-one-vote principle: democratic equality. This principle notwithstanding, as democratic societies became increasingly complex, there also became apparent vast differences in the real socioeconomic power of individuals within these systems. The welfare system—which varies significantly, of course, in its scope from one liberal democratic regime to another— is an attempt to redress the worst effects of class differences upon individuals' lives for the intended benefit of society as a whole. Institutionalized societalism, as embodied in the one-nation-one-vote principle of the United Nations, for example, has the same inherent inadequacy and potential for tension: some states have more power in the world societal system than others, just as some individuals (and strata) have more power in national and subnational social systems.

Very simply, institutionalized societalism, however necessary to legitimate superpower interests in global order, founders on the same hard rocks of gross socioeconomic differences (and their consequences) as does institutionalized individualism. Yet economic—or "structural"—differences in and of themselves do not explain the rise of value-politics. Structural exploitation acts in combination with cultural factors on the one hand, and significant personalities on the other. A field theoretical approach that integrates personality, culture, and social structure is necessary to understand the emergence of effective value-politics. One should expect a religious articulation of political concerns in the global system when there is a combination of: (1) a socioeconomic structure in which there is at one and the same time rising socioeconomic expectations *and* the decline of traditional classes of influence who are being replaced by others, both as a result of mass state-sponsored education (itself a cultural variable, though possibly imposed for structural reasons by a prior colonial power);[3] (2) a cultural history in which religious rhetoric has functioned significantly to define national identity (Shi'ite Islam as a persecuted heterodox sect in historic Persia [contrast Tunisia], the United States as "the nation with the soul of a church" [contrast Canada], South America as the glory of missionary Catholicism, Protestant Northern Ireland, and so on);[4] and (3) a charismatic personality or several charismatic personalities, *called forth by these cultural and structural elements,* committed to more or less the same goals.[5]

SOME HYPOTHESES

These observations lead to several sets of hypotheses. The first has to do with the Robertson-Chirico model itself. We should expect to find that as nation-states that purport to have rational-legal systems of authority increase in their relative position in world society or in their consciousness of their inclusion within the world societal system, value-politics will increasingly characterize political discourse to the extent that this globalization process represents a challenge to the established class *hierarchy* (and not merely to specific established elites). This may occur as a result of either internal religious "renewal" at the hands of claimants to religious traditionalism (e.g., Iran, Northern Ireland) or externally supported consciousness raising (e.g., liberation theology, Islamic *jihad*). Traditional systems of authority (e.g., Saudi Arabia) incorporate value positions definitionally, and thus they will not normally be a source of political destabilization either intra- or internationally. This is also true for societies in which indigenous hierarchical arrangements have been historically minimized (e.g., Iceland, some states of southern Africa). What is problematic about modern value-politics is precisely the introduction of a discussion of particularistic ultimate values into purportedly rational-legal political systems, inasmuch as rational-legal systems presuppose universalistic norms.

The particularistic value-politics problematic thus also raises salient questions about universalistic ultimate values; so the whole topic of value-politics is thrown into high relief by the rise of value particularism. In Robertson and Chirico's terms, then, we should expect to find an association between anthropocentric dualism and value particularism on the one hand, and global telic concerns and value universalism on the other. The confrontation of universalistic value-politics by value particularism forces moderns to recognize that there is, in fact, no value-free politics in much the same way that nuclear weapons has forced us to recognize that there is no value-free science. The class character of "human rights" lies exposed as terror has its own reward.

The second set of hypotheses concerns the relationship between the relative powerfulness of nation-states as actors in the world societal system and both international and intranational value-politics: (1) In comparatively powerful nation-states, leadership elites (e.g., Reagan, Gorbachev) will espouse rhetorics of universalistic ultimate values, whereas intranational groups who perceive themselves as *relatively* deprived will express particularistic ultimate values (e.g., the New Christian Right, Soviet Jews). It is important to emphasize the qualitative nature of relative deprivation, because too often a mistaken emphasis has been placed on quantitative indicators of actual deprivation, and theoretical arguments have become confused. What I am speaking of here are "dying classes," even if they may be perceived by outsiders to be going in style. This quality marks the important interplay between structure and culture, economic resources and life-style. (2) In comparatively weak nation-states within the global system, leadership will espouse the rhetoric of particularistic ultimate values (e.g., the traditionalistic Catholicism of Pinochet), whereas groups who perceive themselves as more deprived will express universalistic ultimate values (e.g., Latin American liberation theology, Polish Roman Catholicism, Palestinians who remain in Israel). (3) Changes in power relationships (whether in the global societal system or a nation-state) will produce comparable changes in the relative articulation of universalistic or particularistic values by different social groups. The more powerful a nation-state becomes within the world societal system, the more likely it is to espouse the rhetoric of universalistic ultimate values (China, the Philippines), other things being equal.

The expression of universalistic ultimate values by national leadership is thus a function of increased power (or perceived increased power) of that nation-state within the world societal system as a whole. Decreases or perceived decreases in power should result in increased particularism. Failure to articulate particularism in such circumstances may well create intranational destabilization as groups who perceive themselves to be among the disenfranchised within the nation-state heighten their expression of particularism vis-à-vis the seemingly nonresponsive power elite. In either case, particularism destabilizes the world societal system. The Ayatollah and Ian Paisley, for example, each crested to power as the result of the failure of a prior regime to deliver on its promises of a better life for nonelites.

Whereas the first set of hypotheses is undergirded by the Robertson-Chirico model, this second set is supported by a theoretical infrastructure that is an extension of work in church-sect theory (including political sectarianism) and the assumption that politics in rational-legal societies has affinities to religion in traditional societies.[6] In prior work, I have offered historical case material to demonstrate that religious organization is tied to both the relative degree of monopolism or pluralism in a social structure within which the organization is operating and its own assessment of its significance within that social structure.[7] In politics, this model translates into something like the following: In a society characterized by superimposition, the dominant power structure would be likely to articulate particularistic value politics (the political equivalent to the "one true church"), attempting to establish and maintain hegemony throughout the sociocultural system. Leaders of dissent, by contrast, would articulate universalistic norms. In a pluralistic society, essentially reversed postures could be assumed—the leadership would articulate universalism, whereas particularism should emanate from dissent, inasmuch as universalism essentially co-opts dissenting movements into its hegemonic structure. At the crux of my church-sect model, however, is also a recognition that as social systems and the organizations within them change, a variety of anomalies can appear, and these anomalous forms may constitute a type-in-themselves, rather than some mere "deviant cases." In a time of intense change, as the post–World War II period may well be in global politics, the anomalous type can garner attention far in excess of its fair share across a broader sweep of history. This is certainly true, for example, of a number of the groups that appeared in revolutionary England, and history may hold it so of our era as well.

The topic of culture, to turn to a third set of potential hypotheses, has not been sufficiently systematically explored. The "explanation" of "cultural differences" has frequently been invoked without adequate attention to exactly what it is that is being explained. As Barrington Moore notes, most "cultural" explanations tend to be circular, not explanations at all.[8] At the same time, to omit culture from an explanatory model is to fall into a crass materialism that time and again has been found wanting. What is clear is that some cultures gravitate around religious symbol systems, whereas others do not. By religious symbol systems I mean coherent rhetorics or discourses that presume a supernatural world inhabited by a sentient being or beings whose character, in the eyes of participants in the action system, has significance beyond the sensible world.[9] Other cultures, though they may well have religious symbol systems, do not gravitate around them in the same way.

A perceptive analysis of this condition is provided by Katherine O'Sullivan See's comparative study of French Canada and Northern Ireland.[10] In both cases, there is a linguistic and religious minority standing over against a linguistic and religious ruling majority. In addition, the ruling majority is the same, and the religions of the two minorities and the two majorities are the same. Yet in French Canada majority opposition gravitated around language, whereas in Northern Ireland it did so around religion. Although not cast in a specifically comparative context, Pétur Pétursson's analysis of the role of language in Icelandic culture as the agent of solidarity—and religion simply as the bearer of that language during the period of colonialism—suggests a picture very similar to the French Canadian one in See's book.[11] By contrast, too little attention is often paid in the Iranian case to the distinction between Persians and Arabs in the Islamic world or to Shi'ite Islam's history of persecution on the one hand and advocacy of revolution on the other.[12] One may likewise suspect, when considering liberation theology, that there are different traditions between Brazil and Argentina, for example, that must be taken into consideration when attempting to explain the presence, absence, or differences among liberation theology movements in these countries. The strong trade union movement in Argentina may well have provided an alternative outlet to democratic impetuses being fostered in Brazil by liberation theology. The proportion of foreign-born clergy and other missionaries in Latin American countries also varies widely.[13]

The interplay of culture and social structure is particularly marked in the phenomenon that Barrington Moore terms "Catonism," and much of what he writes can be applied to the present rise of value particularism.[14] Although it would be a mistake to adopt "Catonism" whole cloth as an "explanation" of value particularism—indeed, it is far more a generalized description than an explanation—it nevertheless provides a pattern for the analysis of cultural elements in several of the politico-religious movements of our time. Observers of Iran and of the New Christian Right will be quick to recognize similarities between Moore's description of the Catonist type and several recurrent themes in these groups' rhetorics. It is important to note, too, that it is not only the moral earnestness of these movements, even the nostalgic elements in their discourses, but their extolling the "virtues of the soil," the great rural ethos, that also ties them to Catonism. In addition, both also strongly emphasize gender differences, female purity, and masculine aggressiveness. What is perhaps more surprising is that the Catonist image also has several affinities with liberation theology rhetoric, raising the question of how genuinely universalistic liberation theology movements are likely to be if and when they in fact obtain some measure of real power.[15]

A final set of hypotheses should center on the charismatic leader or leaders. Although too much may have been made of charisma by students of Third World nationalisms in the 1950s and 1960s,[16] too little attention may be paid today to the psychological anthropology of religious movements, including political religion. The therapeutic emphasis of psychopathological approaches (as witnessed, for example, in the psychological "treatment" afforded in relation to several new religious movements) may put blinders on the contribution of personality to the development of leadership for sociocultural movements such as those we are considering. We need not adopt a naïve "great man" theory of history to recognize that the most successful religiopolitical movements (in terms of the achievement of state power) have been tied to well-recognized leader figures.

In an essay specifically devoted to the relationship between the appearance, success, and failure of charismatic leadership in varying social structures, Ronald Glassman has proposed a series of tentative hypotheses that can be applied to the appearance, success, and failure of religiopolitical movements to the extent that it can be argued that charismatic leadership is an important element in their success.[17] Again, this is not something that can be imposed whole cloth. One limitation of Glassman's approach is that it does not systematically integrate cultural elements into the explanatory structure—although it is obvious from his text that he recognizes they are there and make a difference. Can we not say that just as there are cultural structures that enhance the likelihood that religious elements will become the foci for political action in some societies but not in others, there are cultural structures—which may be in turn the consequence of the priority given to religion among cultural systems—that enhance the likelihood of the appearance of charismatic leadership? Again, Iran's specific devotion to Shi'ite Islam, with its tradition of the holy family, the succession of early imams, and its messianic hope for the return of the Twelfth Imam, jumps immediately to mind. Did not the English heritage of "possessive individualism" contribute at all to the rise of Cromwell?[18] Does not the transformation of millenarianism into manifest destiny contribute to the expectation of a "common man" in the United States rising to restore the fortunes of "lost" Israel? Is there not, in particular, a tie between the premillennialism of much New Christian Right theology and the support of Zionism against Palestinian self-determination and nationhood? Or, to look at the other side of the question: How might Luther's traditionalism rather than Calvin's transforming modernism be related to the cultural system of the German princely states versus independent Geneva?[19] Is liberation theology inhibited in realizing its transforming goals by the tendency of Catholicism to co-opt charisma (if it cannot suppress it)?

This listing of questions suggests varied lines of inquiry into the cultural conditions that surround the emergence of charismatic domination which might profitably be combined with Glassman's structural hypotheses in approaching the problem of religiopolitical movements. Together they display the significance of the topic as one of multiple layers, each of which contributes to the whole. Although these several strata make theory construction more complex, they at the same time make the explanation that arises a more valuable one, and together they demonstrate the relevance and relationship of a religious dimension to an understanding of the political-economic characteristics of world society. There is a kinship, to be sure, between what I am doing here and the analysis by Robert Wuthnow of "World Order and Religious Movements."[20] His seminal essay argues that world order has a structural impact upon the character of religious movements. I quite agree. In addition, however, religious values may have an impact upon world order in conjunction with the relative presence or absence of political-economic power both within nation-states and world society. What makes world society more complicated to analyze, of course, is precisely the two-tiered character of the relationship: the constant presence of the nation-state as an intervening variable.

CONCEPTUAL DEVELOPMENT AND REFINEMENT

In order to elaborate this model further, conceptual development and refinement are necessary in two areas: one involves the use of the term "fundamentalism"; the other relates to the descriptive accuracy of the typological opposition of universalism and particularism.

Fundamentalism

The use of the term "fundamentalism," popular though it is, to conceptualize religiously based value-politics is not without its difficulties. A specific illustrative context for this problematic may be found in Roland Robertson's treatment of Latin American liberation theology.[21] Whereas Robertson provides an insightful and provocative analysis of liberation theology as a sociocultural and sociopolitical movement, his application of the term "fundamentalism" to this movement clearly highlights the pejorative implications of the term. In short, the use of the term "fundamentalism," especially in scholarly discourse, is both deeply negatively value-laden and historically inappropriate. Fundamentalism refers to a very specific movement in Protestant Christianity with well-defined theological tenets. To speak of "Islamic fundamentalism," for example, is to dishonor both faith traditions.[22] The same goes for Catholicism. Indeed, while the New Christian Right in the United States may well be the theological heirs of fundamentalism in its historically specific use, their political agenda has a complex variety of sources. The clearest testimony to this is the inclusion of Roman Catholics and Mormons in New Right cadres—anathematized groups to historic fundamentalism. To label a contemporary religious movement "fundamentalist," then, is in most cases to stigmatize rather than analyze—ironically, the very thing "fundamentalists" themselves are often accused of doing.

If not "fundamentalists," what? I find Eugen Schoenfeld's phrase "militant religion" most helpful.[23] *Militant religion* is religion that denies both the separation of church and state and the superiority of state over church; thus militant religion argues that religion is the basis for national solidarity and social order. Here, now, we can line up Islamic *jihad*, the New Christian Right, Latin American liberation theology, Zionism, Paisleyism, Sikh extremists, and a variety of other movements, both historic and contemporary, of the left and the right. Religious militancy, furthermore, is not an all-or-nothing thing; it comes in varying degrees and waxes and wanes over time. Perhaps it is a sign of our own cultural myopia—or liberal academic biases—that many commentators on current "fundamentalist" movements so quickly forget that the civil rights and anti–Vietnam War movements in the United States both made heavy use of religious rhetoric in their campaigns, as does the anti-apartheid movement *re* the Union of South Africa. Schoenfeld differentiates militant religion into two types: inclusive and exclusive. Liberation theology or the civil rights movement of the 1960s would be inclusive, whereas the New Christian Right or Islamic militancy would be exclusive. Inclusive militancy thus seems to be denoted by universalistic discourses of ultimate values, whereas exclusive militancy is denoted by particularistic discourses. Characteristic of exclusivistic particularism is an insistence upon value conversion (beyond simple political citizenship) before full political benefits can be appropriated.

Universalism and Particularism

This apparent conceptual goodness of fit is marred by the realities of the empirical world. As Lechner, following Robertson, has put it, what we find in the religiopolitical situation of modernity is the paradox "of the particularization of universalism and the universalization of particularism—perhaps the central dynamic in the process of globalization."[24] By this he means that particularistic value systems are generalized to the world arena via universal "rights." In contrast to traditional Saudi Arabia, for example, which enforces religious norms at home but participates in the world oil economy in "value-free" fashion, revolutionary Iran proclaims the extension of Islam to the ends of the earth, and claims not to care about the oil economy.[25] The Union of South Africa, on the other hand, wishes to participate fully in the world-system of states as a "modern" society, while blatantly offending universalistic antiracist values. The New Christian Right in the United States lacks much of the theological precision of historic fundamentalism, but at the same time makes stands on such nonultimate questions as the status of the Panama Canal or Taiwan tests of "faith."

Thus, while one may talk about a dominant trajectory from supernaturalism and particularism to naturalism and universalism on the one hand, in juxtaposition to an alternative "subdominant" mode on the other, the contemporary situation is in fact much more complex and problematic—precisely because of the peculiar combinations of universalistic and particularistic elements in contemporary religiopolitical value networks. These typological difficulties suggest that an alternate mode of conceptualization might prove more theoretically fruitful. I have found the concept of *boundaries* to be a useful construct for integrating the complexity we have observed heretofore.

BOUNDARIES

From the conceptual development of institutionalized societalism out of institutionalized individualism, it can now be argued that analogous scenarios to the gradual transformation of individual religious identity-forming processes in the institutionalized individualism of Western democracies be applied to nation-states in the contemporary world polity, and that on the basis of these, some predictions about the significance of these processes for world order can be made. Religion is one of a number of resources that a group can use to assert (or reassert) and maintain its identity in relation to other corporate actors in the international system, even as it gives transcendent significance to the violation of the taken-for-granted norms of institutionalized societalism by a call for world conversion. The international system of states has come to represent democratic religious pluralism—including the option of "no religion"—writ large: Just as dynamic sects thrive on the options granted to religious organizations by religious pluralism within a liberal democratic society, so specific nation-states can at one and the same time assert their identity as states in the political state pluralism of the United Nations, while at the same time demanding conversion of others as a condition for interaction. The pluralism of institutionalized societalism provides the conditions for religious resurgence largely through the process of *setting boundaries*.

If we look at the whole series of conflicts in the global system of states today, it quickly becomes apparent that boundary claims are at least ostensibly at the center of of many of them. This is not accidental; it follows from the operation of institutionalized societalism in the modern international system of states. A "nation" is *not* in this rationalized world-polity a "people" in the traditional sense. A modern "nation" is a nation-*state*, recognized by other corporate state actors in the system as a corporate actor with *specific boundaries*. Vague boundaries confound the rational character of the one-nation-one-vote system. Institutionalized individualism likewise can be characterized as a boundary-setting process. The Bill of Rights of the United States Constitution sets boundaries, for example, for individuals that the state cannot cross or can cross only under very limited circumstances. The "right to privacy"—much debated recently—is the epitome of this orientation. Whether or not it is a Constitutional guarantee, the right to privacy and other Constitutional rights taken together set bounds that define me vis-à-vis other actors, individual and corporate. As a result of these boundaries, I am at once protected from incursions against my "individuality" and also enabled to assert my "individuality" in a variety of ways. Closely connected to the right to privacy, then, is the "right of self-expression." Many legal cases in the United States involving Constitutional issues are instances of determining either how my individuality is infringed upon by someone else or how I may (or may not) assert my individuality in the face of someone else.

Modernity in its myriad facets represents a series of boundary challenges to nations just as it does to individuals. A simple example: In my brief study of movement leaders in the National Federation of Decency (now the American Family Association), I show how much of these activists' concern about "pornography" has to do with an "invasion" experience.[26] Specific NFD objections do not have to do with sexually explicit materials "in general"; rather, they have to do with the appearance of these materials at the corner store, in motels, and in home television programming. NFD activists see boundaries being challenged—indeed, demolished—in their immediate surroundings. A world has moved in on them, even though they have not moved. Their "individuality" is perceived to be threatened by other—largely corporate—actors crossing significant boundaries. The same type of reaction takes place at the nation-state level over the same phenomenon: Whereas at one time language itself served as a considerable barrier to the distribution of materials that might be termed "pornographic" (i.e., low levels of literacy combined with translation demands), modernity brings with it interstate mails guarantees, the videotape, businesspeople and tourists, all of which violate both personal sexual boundaries and the religiocultural boundaries of historic nations.

Globalization thus challenges a whole series of boundaries even as it provokes the assertion of rights against those boundaries in new and different ways. This is not to say that boundaries have not been transgressed before; the point here, however, is that modernity effectively transgresses all boundaries at once. It challenges social structure, culture, and personality; inasmuch as religion has often served in traditional societies to integrate each of these elements and all of them, the context of the modern international system of states also serves to undermine each and all. Whereas colonization heretofore usually threatened only circumscribed areas of a people's life (extracting raw materials while allowing much indigenous culture to continue, albeit not without some struggle), globalization in the form of institutionalized societalism attacks boundaries of economic self-sufficiency, political power, technology, social class, culture, religion, gender roles, and so on.[27] To be a participant in the global system of states assures nation-states' "rights" in an international democratic pluralism that at the same time throws into stark relief the tensions between the international "haves" and "have nots." Just as one-man-one vote demonstrates the actual powerlessness of the single individual in liberal democratic capitalism, so institutionalized societalism demonstrates the actual powerlessness of the single nation-state in the international system of states.

Religion has frequently served as a response to powerlessness on the part of individuals in liberal democratic states (as well as their historic predecessors). This is not to say that this is the only function of religion, but simply a way religion has in fact functioned. It should come as no surprise, then, that nations as corporate individuals may turn to religion as a vehicle to express frustration against the dominant power cliques in world politics.

Here it should be quite clear that the United States and the Soviet Union have much more in common with each other than any other nation-states. These two states (and their "blocs") form the equivalent of an international two-party system. Both are "secular" states, born of liberal Enlightenment thinking, and both exist as they do by some degree of exploitation of other nations, though of course returning benefits as well. Third parties appear now and then, but they do not succeed: they are either co-opted into the larger two-party system or fall of their own weight. Some nation-states—like some individuals—of course refuse to play the political game at all and retreat to the sidelines to watch the heavyweights slug it out (e.g., Albania, Burma).

In the liberal democratic states, religion has often played an important role in shaping individual identity, even if it has not always effected a public presence. This does not mean that all individuals are religious— or, even less so, equally religious; indeed, individuals may well define themselves as "not religious" (i.e., irreligious or antireligious).[28] Regardless of the pattern of observance, the significance of religion in such pluralistic contexts is that it permits the construction of a symbolic universe of meaning that stands outside the dominant rational world view of a politics of powerlessness (as far as individual actors are concerned). An individual can "be somebody" through a religious mechanism quite apart from the day-to-day routine of a largely meaningless public existence. Some individuals, for a variety of reasons that it is not necessary to adumbrate here, choose to share their religious convictions with others, even "convert" them, and the "right" of freedom of speech gives them wide latitude to do so.[29]

These general conditions can be transferred, *mutatis mutandis*, to the nation in the global system. In a variety of world conflict settings, boundary problems manifest themselves—whether in the specific territorial sense or in the several "symbolic" ways noted earlier. Groups with religious interests see these threatened boundaries charged with a meaning that is quite other than one might expect in "rational" political discourse. Like pornography in the 7-Eleven store, these are not matters to be settled by rational deliberation—indeed, it may well be because of rational deliberation, as the religious person sees it, that matters have come this far. Rather, these are evidences of advances by specific personal forces of evil—Satan by any other name is still Satan—attacking the heart and home of the faithful.

This kind of rhetoric is most obvious, certainly, in Khomeini's Iran, and the Iranian case is perhaps the paradigm of world religious resurgence. But it by no means stands alone. I have here drawn examples from one aspect of the New Christian Right in the United States. Liberation theology in Latin America also arose (whatever may be its reasons for continuing today) as a specific response to boundary incursions— these included the explicitly religious affronts to Roman Catholic hegemony of Marxism and evangelical Protestantism, as well as vast plans of "development," in which traditional land boundaries were violated and population masses resettled (or worse, deprived of normal means of livelihood). At the same time, modern "secular" education replaced institutionalized religious instruction throughout the world, and the ideological focus of the educated was markedly altered. Universal mass education along with demographic shifts crossed long-standing personal and social boundaries.

Northern Ireland, likewise, is a clear case of a modern boundary problem, in which a fictitious definition of Ulster was created ostensibly to protect the Protestant population, but actually served only to accentuate the extent to which Protestant identity in Northern Ireland was a creature of English suzerainty. So, too, "black homelands" in South Africa give the lie to the claim of that nation-state's government to legitimacy precisely because the international system of states will *not* recognize this drawing of boundaries. (That the institutionalized societalism of the international system of states *is* a *new* creation in the world political order is supported by the fact that when the government of the United States placed Native Americans on "reservations," no similar protest was raised. The Native American nations have never been recognized as legitimate nations internationally because they were immobilized before the era of the modern nation-state.)

This is not to say, however, that a resurgence of religious rhetoric automatically accompanies modernization at some evolutionary "stage." Far from it. Iceland, for example, is a nation-state that has undergone as great a degree of modernization as perhaps any other, with its attendant processes of universal education and urbanization; yet there is no sign of the kind of religious resurgence as we see in Iran or Latin America—nor was there ever. A good case can be made, as I have already noted, that language fundamentalism has served as something of a functional equivalent to religious militancy, but without the extremism attendant upon transcendent goals. The Quebec "quiet revolution" is another example. *Religious expressions of national identity arise when religion has historically played a unique role in a people's culture and when that religiousness has been distinctive in terms of national identity.* Shi'ite Islam, for example, is a deviant form of Islam—encompassing no more than 10 percent of the Islamic faithful—yet it is dominant in Iran. Shi'ites have a history of persecution within Islam and at the same time a story of revolution is at the heart of their faith. This also combines with strong messianic expectations and the uniqueness of Persia as a non-Arab nation of historic greatness.

Likewise, although Brazil is by no means the only Latin American country to engender strong movements based in liberation theology, it is also true that its Portuguese heritage gives it distinctiveness among Latin American states. Unlike Argentina, it has lacked a strong labor movement. Compared to Venezuela or even Columbia, it has been weak in democratic overtures. At the same time, it has extensive religious organizational pluralism in both traditional and modern forms, drawing from both native and immigrant cultures. Peru and Bolivia, for example, have significantly different ethnic mixes. Chile, on the other hand, also has a government of repression, as did Brazil during the high tide of its liberation theology movements, and it is not surprising to find Chile currently a center for liberation theology movements. All of Latin America, at the same time, recognizes (at the level of the official church, at least) its unique place in the contemporary Roman Catholic Church, its vanguard position as the demographic center (by population concentration) of Roman Catholicism, but at the same time its dependence upon foreigners for priestly ministry and leadership. The Roman Catholic hierarchy, for its part, is sufficiently historically sophisticated not to lose sight of lessons learned from the Spanish revolution fifty years ago.[30]

Each example, of course, is complex, and important nuances are easily glossed here. The worldwide religious resurgence represents, however, in its myriad forms, an alternate language, a religious language (or discourse), to the language of rational politics. For many, it may be the only language that can be heard on the contemporary scene. It is a vehicle for challenging the assumptions of the Enlightenment—in both its capitalist and socialist variants. Religious discourse in whatever accents is a radical rejection of the Enlightenment principles that led much social science to see religion largely in an accommodationist guise. The resurgence of the languages of ultimacy in politics—as contrasted to penultimate, instrumental values—is an attempt to sit in judgment upon the rational politics of both East and West and call them to account for continued socioeconomic disparities at the level of the global system. Whether in the long run the series of phenomena we are now observing around the globe will have a significant effect on the ordering of world politics remains to be seen; certainly in the short run they are causing some havoc. At the very least this should cause social scientists of religion to have enormous reservations about dismissing religion as an effective variable in political-economic equations or reducing it to a "symbol system" that merely stands for something else that is "real."

THE NEXT STEP: INTERNATIONAL LAW AND SECULARIZATION THEORY

The emergence of the "nation-state" as a legal entity formed the foundation, by the middle of the eighteenth century, for the articulation of positive law, successor to natural law, as the theoretical basis for jurisprudence. By substituting the concrete reality of state sovereignty for the vague referents underlying natural law, positive law provided an empirical, nonultimate solution to the problems of ultimacy inherited by natural law systems from earlier, explicitly religious codes.[31]

Consistent with this development in the law was the appearance of a generalized secularization model applicable to an increasingly wider sphere of human relations. In the "long" eighteenth-century Enlightenment, human beings were first seen and studied as part of the animal world, and human societies were viewed as passing through different stages of development, from the most primitive to the most civilized. The extensive variety in human sociocultural forms thus did not make

human beings unequal, but rather different in their "stage" of development.[32] This posture legitimated the differences among legal systems
that pertained intranationally in the nations of the world. Whereas interference with international processes of world-system expansion
brought the heavy hand of colonialism, intranational laws and customs
were largely respected by colonial powers.

The world of commerce and daily living was thus viewed independently of divine sanction. Such a world view, however, has obvious
limitations, not least of which are its presumption of compliance on the
part of nations around the globe on the one hand, and on the other its
presumption that religious authority systems, already well entrenched,
will accept this definition (i.e., the "privatization" of the religious institution).

The emergence of "institutionalized societalism" after World War II
particularly gave the lie to both these assumptions. While institutionalized societalism transvalues democratic institutionalized individualism
into a principle for global order, it at the same time reintroduces a value
calculus to the law, inasmuch as there is no world organization to function in the same way as the state does to ensure the necessary precon-
ditions for the maintenance of the ideological foundations for democratic
individualism. In particular, institutionalized societalism assumes, at
least for the time being, that nation-state boundaries recognized by the
international system of states are equivalent to "real" nations, merging
the conceptually distinct categories of "nation" and "state."[33] That such
boundaries are often the creation of colonial states for administrative
purposes, rather than the reflection of national sentiment, simply com-
pounds the problem.

Universalistic inclusion in the societal identifications of nation-states,
then, is a specifically modern component of global social processes
founded upon the premises of the secularization model, particularly the
Enlightenment understanding of human "progress" toward "perfec-
tion," defined in Eurocentric terms. At the same time, religious resurgence within nation-states throughout the world casts serious doubts
upon the assumptions of positive law that underlie international law,
just as it does about the validity of secularization theory as an explanation
for change in human behavior with respect to ultimate values. An in-
version takes place such that the reassertion of ultimate values in politics
undermines the positive-law-theory foundation of international law precisely as it demonstrates the actual basis of international law in universalistic natural law which, in turn, lays claim to ultimacy in
articulating its principles.

Thus the paradox "of the particularization of universalism and the
universalization of particularism" results. On the one hand, the militant
movements of religious resurgence in politics are not merely nativistic;

they intend the world as their arena. On the other hand, nation-states like the Union of South Africa appear to accept the standards of the world system of states with respect to religious freedom or the commercial principles of advanced industrial capitalism, but demand the right to adopt particularistic standards of race relations intranationally; yet it is quite clear that the international system of states is not willing to allow this deviance from universalism, largely arguing its case on moral, natural law grounds.

In terms of the interplay of law and religion as sociocultural systems, then, this paradox translates as follows: Religious conceptions of societal inclusivity and exclusivity require legal specification to achieve full institutionalization, while legal specifications require suprapositive, ultimate sanctions. Modern legal study has generally been seen as almost exclusively a "secular" phenomenon. The value assumptions underlying this approach have largely been obscured. The recent religious resurgence in world politics serves as a particularly apt vehicle for explaining these hidden premises and for illuminating the value bases upon which international law and the study of international relations have been constructed. Inasmuch as the two major theoretical paradigms for world order (development and exploitation) are aligned in fundamental presuppositions that give preeminence to economic relationships (i.e., for the development model, capitalism is the key to modernization and its fruits; for the exploitation model, overcoming capitalism is the key to ending exploitation, achieving modernization, and reaping its fruits), the religion-law-politics framework, emphasizing ultimate values, state structures, and national identities, presents a fresh approach to understanding the global sociopolitical situation.

Recent research—for example, by Barrington Moore, Theda Skocpol, or Eric Nordlinger—has demonstrated that the state is a crucial, relatively autonomous component in understanding political change.[34] The state cannot be considered an epiphenomenon to the "real" forces of change. States exist in international systems of states; thus no state system can be fully understood in isolation from the world system of states and state interests that surrounds it. State interests and economic or class interests often have much in common, but not always, and in no case must they be conflated. Furthermore, religion must not be simply lumped together with a series of "communal variables," as Nordlinger does. It is important to see that the law and legal systems react not only to class and power structures, but also to value structures, each of which may function differently in different historical settings.

By the creation of "legal" boundaries in the process of nation-state definition and the treatment of this entity as coequal to national identity, international systems define nationhood as coincident with statehood and generally accept state sovereignty as evidence of nationality. This

relatively artificial definition—often the creation of colonialism—ignores
a host of factors involved in nationhood on the level of participants in
the action system, and by so doing creates a context for religious resurgence as providing the only feasible alternate discourse to legal rationalization. The presumption of secularity by the world order as we
know it underlies the continued maintenance of this societal system; yet
these assumptions totter on weak foundations as soon as they are challenged by a discourse of ultimacy.

A situationalist perspective, as I have advanced elsewhere, argues
that there is potentially a qualitatively significant difference between
religion and other cultural systems.[35] This lies in religion's assertions
about a supernatural world and most specifically in the radical relativization of commonsense notions of life that occur as a result of religious
doctrines of life-after-death. The doctrine of the afterlife, coupled with
religious militancy, greatly enhances the potential for violence on the
part of religious actors. That this is true is evidenced in the relative
absence of violence among groups where dissent is articulated in rhetorics that are nonreligious (e.g., the French Canadians). The introduction
of religious symbol systems into situations of conflict manifestly increases the intensity of the conflict, as religious devotees become convinced of the *eternal* rightness of their cause. This may be seen very
clearly in the Iran-Iraq War (on the Iranian side) and in Islamic *jihad*
generally.

Because nation-states exist in international systems of states and because religion does give expression to suffering, destabilizing value-
politics are likely to persist in world society as long as there remain
significant gaps between rich and poor nations, and between rich and
poor peoples within nations. The greatest likelihood for universalistic
ultimate values to advance within world society is for a nation-state to
be relatively strong within the world societal economy but to have relatively little political-economic disparity among its people (e.g., the Scandinavian countries) and little displacement of its historic class hierarchy
(to the extent that there is one) as a result of socioeconomic change. The
greatest danger for destabilization is during shifts upward in international power that are not reflected in across-the-board improvements in
social power for the citizenry (e.g., Iran under the Shah).

At the same time, it must be recognized that value-politics itself is
likely to continue to be a part of the global societal system—that is,
the language of values is likely to continue to be the way the dispossessed of the world articulate grievances *and* the way the powerful of
the world articulate hegemony. Specifically, in world societal politics
universalistic value positions embody ideology just as much as particularistic ones. This has generally been recognized by the superpow-
ers about opposing systems, but not about their own. Contemporary

rhetorics of universal value are always articulated from a position in relation to other positions. "Human rights," for example, always carries within it a socially based definition of "humanity," which is precisely why the leadership of the United States and the Soviet Union and the Vatican and so on can each claim to be acting in support of "human rights" in spite of peculiar actions by any one (or several) in Nicaragua, South Africa, Israel-Palestine, Afghanistan, Czechoslovakia, and so on.

One can, finally, bring generalizations from the sociology of religion to bear on the resolution of crises of value particularism. The argument can be made that the strongest long-term base for removing tension over value differences is greater parity in the world socioeconomic order. Sectarianism declines in social significance as sectarians cease to be socioculturally and politically-economically dispossessed. Charismatic leadership is inherently unstable, and its routinization largely depends upon outside forces. The absence of a lively sociopolitical religious sectarianism occurs in those nation-states where religious dissidents do not experience perceived socioeconomic discrimination (e.g., Scandinavia), and increases where the obverse is true (e.g., Northern Ireland, Palestine, India's Sikhs, Sri Lanka's Tamils). It should be clear from what I have said earlier that I am not trying to argue a simple materialism here— that ultimate values are *merely* a function of political-economic power. I am trying to suggest, however, that the expression of specific kinds of ultimate values goes hand in hand with position in the political-economic structure of society—whether national society or global society—as mediated by culture and leadership potential. The appearance of ultimate values in the language of global societal politics (e.g., the quest for a World Islamic Order) is itself a function of the increasing awareness of global society as a society, much as the religious squabbles of the Reformation period were associated with a major shift into nation-states from the medieval period. Universalism and particularism are inherent in all value systems (hence universalistic particularism and particularistic universalism); emphases upon one or the other value posture covary with other sociocultural variables in specific social situations. I have tried to indicate the contexts in which particularistic religious militancy is most likely to emerge and some of the factors that may lead to its diffusion.

6

Religious Transformation and Social Conditions: A Macrosociological Analysis

James T. Duke and Barry L. Johnson

How do religions change, and why do such changes take place? What social conditions are conducive to religious change, and what conditions facilitate maintenance of the status quo? Are some religions more susceptible to growth or decline than others, and what accounts for these differences between religions? Is a decline in the established religion accompanied by growth in alternative religions? Are people becoming irreligious, and is religion losing its influence in the social world? These are some of the most crucial questions in the study of contemporary world religions. Through a comparative study of religious change in two hundred nations, we give some tentative answers to these questions in this chapter.

Indications of religious change are found in virtually every nation. In recent years, in Great Britain more than a hundred Anglican churches have been declared "redundant" each year, and there has been lively debate about how best to use these buildings.[1] In Bulgaria, many beautiful cathedrals and chapels are now used for museums and office buildings. In Africa, the number of Christians has grown from 10 million in 1900 to 203 million in 1980.[2] The number of Christians in the world increased at a rate of 1.4 percent per year between 1815 and 1914, but has declined since 1914. This decline began slowly, but has increased to about 1 percent per year.[3] In the United States, religion in "Middletown, USA" seems stronger today than it was in the 1920s.[4] Yet over 20 percent of the world's population, or roughly 1 billion people, are nonreligious or atheistic.

EXPLANATIONS OF RELIGIOUS CHANGE

One way to explain religious change is to treat it as a normal component of the culture and social structure of a society and to invoke established theories of social change to account for it. Many explanations of social change have been offered, including conflict, economic, cyclical, evolutionary, ecological, social-psychological, and equilibrium models.[5] Processes such as invention, diffusion, social strain, differentiation, social movements, and innovation may apply to religion as well as other aspects of social life. Specifically religious processes, such as profanation, politicization, reform or renewal, repression of competing religions, and obsolescence of a particular religion also need to be encompassed in a comprehensive theory of religious change.

Secularization Theory and Its Critics

The most frequently used explanation of religious change is secularization theory, which we will also use as our own starting point. Secularization theory posits an overall decline of religion and religious influences because of a set of specific conditions related to industrialization and modernization, including economic development, rationality, and the growth of scientific thinking. Daniel Bell has provided a succinct statement of the nature and cause of secularization that allows us to address some of the theoretical and conceptual issues surrounding secularization theory:

At the end of the eighteenth and to the middle of the nineteenth century, almost every Enlightened thinker expected religion to disappear in the twentieth century. The belief was based on the power of Reason. Religion was associated with superstition, fetishism, unprovable beliefs, a form of fear. . . . From the end of the nineteenth century to the middle of the twentieth century, almost every sociological thinker . . . expected religion to disappear by the onset of the twenty-first century.[6]

Secularization theorists usually make four interrelated assumptions about the nature and causes of secularization: (1) secularization is linear; (2) once begun, secularization is inevitable; (3) the root cause of secularization is modernization, and it is therefore a recent phenomenon; and (4) secularization is primarily a phenomenon of Western culture and the Enlightenment. Sharot, Ayalon, and Ben-Rafael summarize this point of view: "Secularization . . . has commonly been viewed either as a dimension or as a consequence of modernization; industrialization, urbanization, the growth of science and technology, the spread of education, the development of the mass media, and the participation of the masses into political society have been seen as contributing factors in the decline of religion."[7]

The scope of this chapter will not allow us to review the works of the many secularization theorists to show in detail how these assumptions are elaborated in each one's writings.[8] We also do not intend to imply that everyone who has ever written on secularization makes any or all of these assumptions. We do argue, however, that most who have written on secularization see it essentially in this light.[9]

Recently, serious questions have been raised concerning secularization theory, and the data presented here will raise further challenges. Stark and Bainbridge's work represents the best-known attempt to challenge some of the extreme assumptions of secularization theory.[10] They argue that secularization is a self-limiting process and that new religions develop to fill the void when a traditional religion loses its influence in society. Robertson and Chirico and Lechner have recently noted the "resurgence" or "revitalization" of religion both in the United States and worldwide.[11]

The four assumptions of secularization theory are largely unwarranted from the data on religious change and are not necessary for the explanation of "secularization." Our data lead to a different set of conclusions about the nature of religious change: (1) religious change is sometimes cyclical rather than linear; (2) religious reformations through attempts to strengthen religion occur frequently; (3) the decline in influence of a dominant religious tradition is almost always accompanied by the rise of an alternative religious tradition; (4) religious change is found in virtually every society in the world and is evident in the earliest historical accounts; (5) religious change almost inevitably accompanies other (especially political) sociocultural changes.

Secularization, like religion, has been defined in many different ways, and many different indicators of secularization have been proposed. Initially we will define secularization as a decline in the strength of a religious tradition. Later in this chapter we will use a more specific definition of secularization as the replacement of religion by irreligion. In the first sense, secularization is likely to begin early in the history of the tradition and to be a continuing problem to its leaders and adherents. Biblical references to people straying from established religious norms are at least as old as the Cain and Abel story. Renewal and reform, then falling away, are repeated over and over again. For example, in the history of the kingdom of Judah between 975 BCE. and 587 BCE., there are *five* definite cycles of apostasy and reform (see 1 Kings 12–22, 2 Kings 1–25).

Forces working toward secularization and decline are opposed by other forces toward renewal and recommitment. Often one set of forces is stronger than the other, but typically neither of these "dual tendencies" is strong enough to overcome and eliminate its opposite.[12] Decline in the strength of one religion is almost always accompanied by growth in the strength of other religions. Only in very recent years, and only in Marxist nations, have the majority of citizens in any nation been nonreligious.

This means that the process of religious transformation is almost never inexorable or inevitable. While it is sometimes linear, it is also sometimes cyclical or unpredictable. This is not to deny the existence of definite patterns in religious transformation: we shall demonstrate amazingly stable patterns with our own data. But such patterns are complex, flexible, and issue from diverse causes. We can only begin to unravel these patterns in this chapter.

Obviously, social change is very complex, and many sociological theories and concepts may be useful in its explanation. It is our view that secularization theory can account for some aspects of religious change. What is needed eventually is an integrated theory that brings together the several strands of secularization theory, church-sect theory, religious processes, and social-change theory. Such a theory must be grounded in empirical data on religious change drawn from many time periods and diverse cultures.

The major goals of this chapter are (1) an examination of macrosociological data concerning worldwide religious change between 1900 and 1980, (2) an empirical assessment of the utility of secularization theory in explaining religious change, and (3) the formulation of a tentative set of explanations for these changes.

The Processes of Religious Change

A long list of social processes by which religious transformation is accomplished could be made. Here we seek to elucidate a rather restricted number of processes that have the greatest applicability to religious change. Many of these have been treated at length in the sociological literature with reference to social change in general, and the first two processes are the major ones addressed in the secularization paradigm. Our discussion of these processes will necessarily be brief and largely definitional.

Differentiation. Religion is separated from other aspects of social life. Specifically religious organizations, structures, and social roles are created, and religion becomes autonomous. Differentiation of specifically religious values and beliefs occurs.

Profanation. A decline of religious belief occurs. Religious teachings are challenged and sometimes replaced. The number of people who adhere to religious beliefs declines.

Resistance and Reform. Religious people resist profanation and attempt to strengthen religious beliefs and commitment. Revival and awakening characterize the religious life of the community.

Diffusion. New religious ideas are imported from another society. New denominations, beliefs, and practices are passed from one culture to another.

Politicization. Religion is brought into the political arena and becomes a political issue. One religion may become the state religion, and adherence to it becomes a political duty or asset. The power of the government may be used to support some and suppress other manifestations of religion.

Repression. The political structure of the society is used to destroy or repress manifestations of religion. Many aspects of religion become politically unacceptable or dangerous, and religious organizations and people move underground.

Obsolescence. Traditional, institutional forms of religion and belief become obsolescent. Support for religion or for some denominations and practices declines. Churches fail to meet the changing needs of individuals, and people look elsewhere for meaning.

Innovation. New denominations arise, and new interpretations of old doctrines or rituals occur. Religion becomes renewed and better adapted to changing social conditions and needs. Innovation may result from reformist movements of a sectlike character or from entirely new revelations or creations.

THE CYCLE OF RELIGIOUS TRANSFORMATION

In this chapter we formulate a tentative model of religious change that incorporates the processes of secularization and decline, as well as processes of growth, reform, and replacement of a declining religion with a growing religion. The model can best be described as a cycle encompassing four stages, with the cycle capable of being repeated several times. Figure 6.1 represents this cycle graphically.

The stages of the cycle are these: (1) *decline,* during which the established religion loses influence, and new religions originate and evolve to challenge the old one; (2) *dominance,* in which a growing religion (or denomination) gains the position of a majority religion (either through the displacement of a formerly dominant religion or through ascendance over several other competing religions); (3) *sustained growth,* in which the new majority religion consolidates its gains and increases its influence; and (4) *transition,* in which the majority religion peaks in influence and begins to decline. Since this process is cyclical, decline occurs again (Stage Five is a repeat of Stage One), and the process continues indefinitely.

To describe this cycle of religious change and identify some of its key

Figure 6.1
The Cycle of Religious Transformation

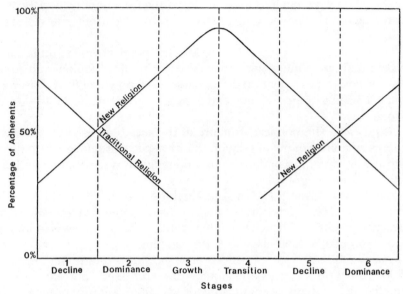

components, it would be instructive to be able to go back historically to the time when religion first became institutionalized, to see what society might have been like "before religion," so to speak, but such historical records are not available. The first condition we can identify in the earliest and least-developed societies is one in which religion is integrated into the culture of the society and intertwined in a robust way with nearly every aspect of life.[13] There is a unitary system of beliefs and practices, and no separate denominations exist. Religious socialization is part of cultural socialization, no conversion to new religions occurs, and limited apostasy is possible. Little differentiation of religious structure from social structure is present. This model of primitive religion perhaps may be fairly accurate, but it is too stereotypic and idealized to serve as anything but a model by which to contrast religious changes.[14]

As primitive societies become more modern, or as they come into contact with modern societies, the traditional religion tends to lose its hold on the lives of its members, and a process of religious change sets in. This weakening of the majority religion begins very early in the history of a society, and in Europe obviously began much earlier than the Enlightenment. Thus, explanations of secularization that depend on

"Enlightenment" reasoning, such as Durkheim's, are superficial if not incorrect.[15]

As social change proceeds, new religious beliefs and practices are introduced—either from other groups (such as from the Philistines to ancient Israel) or from the creation of new religious expressions indigenous to the culture. Decline in the majority religion, therefore, is accompanied by the growth of new denominations or religions. In many cases, denominational differentiation is magnified, and extensive conversion occurs in this stage.

In this part of the cycle there tends to be a weaker commitment by people to traditional ways, including the original, established religion. Frequently the conflict between the old and new religions is intense and bitter, and the competition often provokes periods of renewal, reform, and recommitment to the traditional religion. Sometimes revitalization is remarkably successful, and sometimes it represents only a delaying action with little lasting influence. Because religious conflict is high and new denominations are being created, the government is frequently drawn into the conflict, and religion becomes politicized.

History suggests, and our data verify, that traditional indigenous (what Barrett calls "tribal") religions have little staying power after they come into contact with new, proselytizing "world" religions. Indigenous religions in ancient Egypt, India, China, and Africa eventually gave way to more "modern" expressions of religion such as Christianity, Islam, and Buddhism. The original religion was discarded, lost, and eventually forgotten. However, Barrett also correctly notes that tribal religion in the immediate past century has shown more resistance to extinction than anyone anticipated.[16]

Religion itself does not die with the old religion. Instead, it is replaced by a new religion that in many ways is adhered to just as strongly as was the traditional one. The new religion experiences a period of growth and strengthening which may continue for many decades. This usually results in the new religion gaining substantial dominance in a nation, often approaching or exceeding 90 percent of the populace. But eventually, this religion, too, begins to lose strength, a transition to decline occurs, and the stages are repeated.

There is little historical evidence that this cycle is repeated more than a very few times, but we would argue that there is much evidence from scriptural and historical sources for the existence of such cycles of religious transformation. Later in this chapter we will present some statistical evidence for the occurrence of the cycle.

This cycle of religious transformation may be viewed as a process of "thawing" and "refreezing." The entire cultural tradition that supported the traditional religion, once frozen into a strong institutional order, tends to lose its strength, to defrost, and to become less powerful and influential in the lives of its adherents. As this process occurs, however, a new religion is originated, becomes institutionalized or "frozen," and supplants the old religion.

Although we have described this process of transformation as cyclical, we do not wish to imply that the process is inevitable or inexorable. Societies may move in either direction along the cyclical line. History is full of examples of societies in which a dominant religion experienced rebirth, renewal, and an infusion of new enthusiasm and strength. These periods of renewal are often short-lived and accompanied by political trends or events which support them. Our data will show that there are a few societies presently in a stage of reform and renewal, and this has occurred frequently in the past as well, though we do not have the kinds of data necessary to document it quantitatively.

One virtue of our cyclical approach is that "secularization" is incorporated into the model. Rather than attributing a decline of the majority religion to modernization, we hypothesize that it is a normal tendency of all majority religions to grow and then decline, and this is probably as likely to occur in premodern nations as in modern ones. Our model allows us to explain much of the data supporting the secularization paradigm without accepting the assumptions of linearity, inevitability, modernity, and Westernization that usually accompany secularization theory.

Method

Data for this study were obtained from David Barrett's *World Christian Encyclopedia* (1982). Barrett and his colleagues, in a monumental research effort, gathered data on the religious and denominational preferences of people in 224 nations throughout the world. Each nation's populace is enumerated by major religious classification, such as Christians, Buddhists, Jews, Nonreligious, and Atheists. Christians are subdivided into a number of categories, including Roman Catholics, Protestants, Marginal Protestants, Catholic Pentecostals, and Anglicans. For each major religious group, the number of adherents is reported for 1900, mid–1970, mid–1975, and projected to the years 1980 and 2000. Also reported is the annual rate of change from 1970 to 1980 through both natural increase and conversion.

Some figures are reported exactly, while others are obviously estimated to the nearest thousand. Although the *Encyclopedia* was published in 1982, the enumerations were done in the mid–1970s. We have no independent way of evaluating the accuracy of these figures internationally, with one exception. An accurate listing is available of church membership of the Church of Jesus Christ of Latter-day Saints (Mormon) for many nations of the world.[17] Barrett's figures for this denomination seem to represent its membership fairly, although some of his figures lag behind actual membership by several years.

Obviously there are many difficulties in such an undertaking, and we have no doubt that there are inaccuracies in Barrett's data. But the enumerations were painstakingly done and represent the best current estimates of religious adherents worldwide. Thus we have concluded that Barrett's figures are sufficiently accurate approximations of religious adherence to permit comparative trend analysis.

The stages of religious transformation were measured as follows: (Stage One) *Decline*—the percentage of adherents to the majority religion (over 50 percent of the population) was smaller in 1970 than in 1900, the number of converts between 1970 and 1980 was negative, and the GNP per capita for the nation was under $3,500; (Stage Two) *Dominance*—the majority religion in 1900 was replaced by another majority religion by 1970, the number of converts to the new majority religion between 1970 and 1980 was positive, and the GNP per capita was under $3,500; (Stage Three) *Sustained Growth*—the percentage of adherents to the majority religion was greater in 1970 than in 1900, and the number of converts between 1970 and 1980 was positive; (Stage Four) *Transition*—the percentage of adherents to the majority religion was greater in 1970 than in 1900, but the number of converts between 1970 and 1980 was negative (more people left than joined the majority religion); (Stage Five) *Decline*—the same as Stage One, except the GNP per capita was over $3,500; (Stage Six) *Dominance*—the same as Stage Two, except the GNP per capita was over $3,500.

Nations in the "reform" stage, which do not fit the cyclical model, showed a decline in the percentage of adherents to the majority religion between 1900 and 1970, but a positive number of converts between 1970 and 1980.

Each nation was classified into one of the four stages of religious transformation, with the first two stages repeated for modern nations, to see in broad perspective the changes that have occurred from 1900 to 1980. Much is missed, however, since we have no data on religious changes between 1900 and 1970. Thus, while we can see broad changes, Barrett's data do not allow us to view the microreligious changes in each nation. Since our approach is macrosociological, however, the data are useful for our purposes and enable us to make some significant conclusions concerning broad religious transformations over about an eighty-year period.

Some "nations" that Barrett included in the *World Christian Encyclopedia* were excluded from our own analysis. Specifically, any nation with a population of less than 10,000 was excluded because we considered these units to be too small for valid change statistics to be computed. These excluded small nations and territories are: Anquilla, British Antarctic Territories, British Indian Ocean Territories, Canton and Enderbury Islands, Christmas Island, Cocos Islands, Falkland Islands, French Southern and Antarctic Territories, the Holy See (Vatican City State), Johnston Island, Midway Islands, Nauru, Niue Island, Norfolk Island, Pitcairn Islands, St. Helena, St. Pierre and Miquelon, Svalbord and Jan Mayen Islands, Tokelau Islands, Turks and Caicos Islands, Tuvalu, Wake Island, and Wallis and Futuna Islands.

Many dependent colonies were included as "nations," even though they do not enjoy independent political status. Our data-set thus encompasses two-hundred nations representing virtually every major political unit in the world. The basic data for this study are found in the appendix to this chapter. Each nation was classified according to its stage of religious transformation, and the percentage of adherents to the majority religion in 1900 and 1970 is reported. The yearly rate of change by conversion (both into and out of a religion) are reported for the decade between 1970 and 1980, the only decade for which such information is available. These data can be subjected to other types of analyses, and we hope that they will be found a valuable resource for use by other researchers.

Religious Change by Geographical Area

The number of nations in each stage, classified by geographical area, is shown in Table 6.1. The largest number (62), some third of all nations, were found in Stage One, the stage of decline. As we have defined it, this stage includes only poorer nations with a GNP per capita less than $3,500. Stage Five includes those nations with a GNP over $3,500 in which the majority religion is in decline. When we add the 27 nations in this stage to those in Stage One, we have 89 nations, nearly 45 percent of the total, in which the majority religion was in steady decline between 1900 and 1980.

Stages Two and Six represent situations in which the original majority religion was replaced by another majority religion (or irreligion) between 1900 and 1970. There are 48 nations in Stage Two (with a GNP under $3,500) and another 8 in Stage Six (GNP over $3,500). The 56 nations in these two stages represent 28 percent of all nations in our study.

Twenty-one nations in Stage Three exhibited steady growth by the majority religion between 1900 and 1980, and another 26 nations in Stage Four are just reaching the peak and beginning to decline. Finally, 8 nations are in the stage of "reform." They showed a decline between 1900 and 1970, but between 1970 and 1980 the majority religion increased (very slightly) through conversion.

In looking at the geographical distribution of nations in each stage,

Table 6.1
Number of Nations in Each Stage, by Geographical Area

REGION	1	2	STAGES 3	4	5	6	Reform	PERCENT DECLINING*
North Africa	4	2	6	4	0	0	2	33%
South Africa	9	29	1	1	0	0	0	95
Caribbean	14	1	3	1	2	0	0	81
Central America	7	1	0	0	0	1	0	100
South America	6	1	2	3	0	0	1	54
Southeast Asia	4	4	3	5	2	0	0	56
South Asia	2	0	2	3	0	0	2	22
Oceania	5	8	0	1	3	0	0	94
Middle East	6	1	1	5	0	1	2	50
Eastern Europe	1	1	1	1	3	2	1	70
Western Europe	4	0	2	2	16	3	0	85
North America	0	0	0	0	1	1	0	100
TOTAL	(62)	(48)	(21)	(26)	(27)	(8)	(8)	72%

* Percentage of nations in which the majority religion in 1900
experienced a decline (Stages 1, 2, 5, & 6).

what stands out in Table 6.1 are the large numbers of Caribbean nations in Stage One, African nations in Stage Two, and European nations in Stage Five. A decline in the formerly dominant religious traditions in South Africa, the Caribbean, Central America, Europe, and North America is very notable.

On the other hand, the nations in Stages Three and Four are most likely to be found in North Africa, South or Central Asia, and the Middle East. These same areas also have the largest number of nations undergoing religious growth or reform after a previous decline.

These trends become even more notable when we examine the percentage of nations in which the majority religion experienced a decline (combining Stages One, Two, Five, and Six), also presented in Table 6.1. Over 90 percent of the nations of North America, South Africa, Central America, and Oceania have experienced a decline of the majority religion since 1900, and decline has occurred in the majority religion in over 80 percent of the nations in Western Europe and the Caribbean. Those areas that exhibit the greatest stability of the majority religion are South Asia, South America, and the Middle East nations having religions with moderate stability. We should note also that 72 percent of the nations in our study can be classified as experiencing decline or displacement of the traditional religion since 1900.

These data suggest a powerful conclusion concerning the applicability of secularization theory to religious decline. Some of the areas where the decline of the majority religion is most evident are indeed modern industrial nations. But the majority of nations experiencing decline are premodern nations that have had relatively rapid rates of social and economic change but still remain far behind in economic development. We suggest that it is the *process* of social change, including the process of modernization, that causes religious change, *not* the condition of modernization (or having achieved modernization) itself. Secularization is a process that occurs in the least-developed societies as well as in modern societies, and is due not to an achieved level of scientific thought or materialistic comfort, but rather to fundamental processes and experiences of change. These changes are likely to bring into question the applicability of an old religion to changing times as well as foster the introduction of new ideas, beliefs, and denominations (structures).

In most of the nations where the majority religion is in decline, many other religions are growing. Focusing on the majority religion, therefore, as we have in Table 6.1, does not give a fair indication of the strength of religion as a whole.

What Religions Are Most Subject to Decline?

Nations can also be classified according to the majority religion of the nation and the stage of religious transformation (see Table 6.2). Large numbers of Catholic, Protestant, and tribal religions are found in Stage One, the stage of decline. The great majority of nations with a tribal (indigenous) religion are in Stage Two, suggesting that tribal religion is susceptible to replacement by another religion. Only Singapore exhibited growth in the number of adherents to the indigenous (Chinese Folk) religion during the period between 1900 and 1980. Decline is also characteristic of Christian nations, especially Protestant ones.

Conversely, Muslim, Buddhist, and Hindu faiths show the greatest resistance to decline, although the percentage of nations exhibiting stability (63 percent vis-à-vis 50 percent) should not give the leaders of these religions much cause for celebration. The staying power of these religions derives in part from legal restrictions both on individuals changing religions and on legal proselyting by other religions in many countries where they are dominant.

An important theoretical question is why tribal and Protestant religions have suffered such decline. Political causes are certainly to blame for much of this decline, especially in the former colonial nations in which tribal religion is found. As we have shown elsewhere, colonial

Table 6.2
Number of Nations in Each Stage, by Majority Religion

RELIGION	STAGES 1	2a	2b	3	4	5	6a	6b	Reform	PERCENT DECLINE*
Catholic	23	2	8	6	9	11	1	0	2	69%
Protestant	13	5	5	1	0	14	4	1	0	97
Orthodox	2	0	1	0	1	0	2	0	0	80
Muslim	11	1	2	8	10	0	1	0	5	36
Tribal	10	38	0	0	1	1	0	0	0	98
Buddhist	2	0	0	0	4	1	0	0	1	38
Hindu	1	1	0	1	1	0	0	0	0	50
Jewish	0	0	0	0	0	0	0	1	0	--
Minorities	0	1	27	5	0	0	0	5	0	--
Non-Religious	0	0	5	0	0	0	0	1	0	--
(N)	(62)	(48)	(48)	(21)	(26)	(27)	(8)	(8)	(8)	72%

* Percentage of nations in which the majority religion in 1900 experienced a decline (Stages 1, 2, 5 & 6).

Religious Stability = 100 - % decline.

a = in 1900.

b = in 1970

nations sometimes suppressed and sometimes tolerated the indigenous religions in their colonies, but their dominant political influence enabled proselyting by other denominations, usually the majority religion in the colonial nations, as well as discrediting the indigenous religion. The growth of Christianity and the accompanying decline in tribal religion in African nations is especially notable.[18]

The relative decline in those nations where Protestantism was the majority religion prior to 1900 is probably due to those factors to which secularization theorists often point: growth of a secular culture, replacement of faith by scientific analysis, and concern with materialistic rather than spiritual values. Still, the freedom of religion typical of Protestant nations may account for the decline of the majority religion better than modernization itself, a theme to which we will return in Chapter 8.

Replacement of One Religion by Another

Staying power against the onslaught of new religions is one thing; the ability to gain majority status by replacing another religion is quite

Table 6.3
Religions Gaining Majority Status in a Nation, 1900–1970

RELIGION	PERCENTAGE
TOTAL SAMPLE (N = 55)	
Christian	25%
Catholic	(14)
Protestant	(11)
Jewish	2
Muslim	4
Nonreligious	11
Minorities (no majority religion)	58
TOTAL	100%
WITH MINORITY RELIGIONS REMOVED (N = 23)	
Christian	61%
Catholic	(35)
Protestant	(26)
Muslim	9
Jewish	4
Nonreligious	26
TOTAL	100%

a different thing. Table 6.3 shows which religions have gained majority status during the years 1900 to 1970. In almost 60 percent of these cases the majority religion was replaced by several minority religions. When we eliminate these cases, we are left with twenty-three nations in which one religion (or irreligion) replaced another. In 61 percent of these nations, it was a Christian denomination that gained majority status. Most of this replacement took place in Africa under the influence of colonial rule. Also notable is the fact that six of these twenty-three nations are Marxist regimes in which nonreligion or atheism replaced the established religion.

What is perhaps most remarkable is that religions with the most staying power (Islam, Buddhism, Hinduism) had very little success in gaining ascendance over previously established religions. Although these faiths are strongly institutionalized in their own areas, they have not spread as have Christianity and irreligion.

Christianity, then, is subject to replacement by other religions but has also been the major religion replacing others during the past century. More attention to specific denominations would flesh out this picture of the dynamics of the growth and decline of the Christian religion.

The Growth of Atheism and Irreligion

One of the major arguments of secularization is that as modernization proceeds, religion is replaced by irreligion or atheism and by a set of secular values and beliefs that provide no place for religion.[19] This is a more narrow definition of secularization than we have been using in this chapter. Peter Berger, for example, argues that secularization means "that the modern West has produced an increasing number of individuals who look upon the world and their own lives without the benefit of religious interpretation."[20] Perhaps the best test of secularization theory, then, might be a growth in the number of people who are nonreligious and/or atheist.[21]

The percentage of the populace of each nation who are irreligious (either nonreligious or atheist), as reported by Barrett, is shown in Table 6.4. Of the 200 nations in this study, Barrett found no irreligious people in 36 nations. We must admit that there is a good probability that there is *somebody* in each of these nations who is either atheist or nonreligious, but we agree with Barrett that the number is so small as to be insignificant.

In every other nation in the world except Uruguay, the number of irreligious people has grown since 1900. In 87 nations, fewer than 1 percent of the population are irreligious, and in 33 nations between 1 and 3 percent are irreligious. On the other hand, there are 22 nations with more than 10 percent either atheistic or nonreligious. Thirteen of these nations have Marxist governments and ideologies. Five of the remaining 9 are industrialized nations of Western Europe (France, West Germany, Sweden, Netherlands, Italy), and 2 are among the most modern nations in eastern Asia (Japan and Hong Kong). Australia is also an industrialized nation with a Western Protestant heritage, and Uruguay is one of the most modern and Westernized nations in Latin America, with a long antireligious heritage.

We suggest that modernization is not in itself a very compelling explanation for the growth of irreligion in these nations, especially the Marxist nations. In fact, it is in some of the least industrialized Marxist nations (Albania, Mongolia) that atheism is most prevalent. The suppression of religion in these nations is primarily ideological and political and has little relationship to modernization or Western values.

Table 6.4

Percentage of the Population Who Are Nonreligious or Atheist, by Region, 1980

		PERCENTAGE WHO ARE NON-RELIGIOUS OR ATHEISTS					
REGION	NONE	0.01–0.99	1.00–2.99	3.00–9.99	10.00+	TOTAL	(N)
North Africa	28%	67%	6%	0%	0%	101%	(18)
South Africa	33	63	2	2	0	100	(40)
Middle East	13	56	31	0	0	100	(16)
East & SE Asia	11	33	6	17	33	100	(18)
South & Cent Asia	33	56	11	0	0	100	(9)
Oceania	29	47	0	18	6	100	(17)
Caribbean	14	33	38	10	5	100	(21)
Central America	0	67	33	0	0	100	(9)
South America	0	46	38	8	8	100	(13)
North America	0	0	0	100	0	100	(2)
Western Europe	11	11	30	30	18	100	(27)
Eastern Europe	0	10	0	10	80	100	(10)
PERCENT IN EACH STAGE	18	44	16	11	11	100	(200)
TOTAL (N)	(36)	(87)	(33)	(22)	(22)	---	(200)

Even in those nations, however, where religion has been most severely suppressed (in Albania a priest was executed for baptizing an infant), there is evidence that religion still retains vitality in the minds of the people.[22] This provides partial support for Stark and Bainbridge's argument that secularization is a self-limiting process.

If the secularization thesis is applied only to Western nations, we still find some pairs of nations with very similar geographic location and levels of industrial development that have different levels of irreligion. Specific cultural, historical, and political factors have probably been at work in each of these cases. For example, in Sweden 17.0 percent of the people were classified as nonreligious and another 11.7 percent as atheist. Its next-door neighbor, Norway, had only 1.2 percent nonreligious and 0.5 percent atheist. Part of this difference may be due to measurement errors, but surely the level of modernization or the presence of scientific thought are not so different in these nations as to produce such great differences in irreligion. Other instructive comparisons may be

Table 6.5
Characteristics of Nations in Each Stage

Stage	Median Yearly Rate of Change Between 1970 and 1980	Median GNP Per Capita in 1979
1	-.0012	$ 980
2	-.0233	485
3	+.0003	1200
4	-.0003	1010
5.	-.0023	6375
6	-.0017	7063
Reform	+.00005	775

made between Uruguay and either Paraguay or Argentina, between Japan and South Korea, or between France and Belgium. Again, too, we need to reiterate that political causes, specifically the political influence of a leftist ideology, have had great influence in the majority of nations with relatively high proportions of irreligion.

The Rate of Change: The Exponential Hypothesis

The median rate of change between 1970 and 1980 for the nations in each stage of religious transformation is shown in Table 6.5. Religious growth is very slow in Stage Three, and religious decline, which is just beginning to occur, is also very slow in Stage Four. Stages One, Five, and Six show fairly significant rates of decline, which amount to about 1 percent change every four to eight years. The greatest rate of decline in a religion is found in Stage Two, where a former majority religion has already been replaced by another religious tradition. The old religion is declining very rapidly, over 2 percent per year on the average.

These findings suggest that as a nation's religion reaches a peak and begins to decline, the rate of decline is at first very slow. However, this decline begins to gain momentum as the majority religion loses adherents and reaches a very high rate of decline after having been replaced by another religion. This exponential curve of religious change is one of the most significant findings of the present study. It implies that once a religious tradition has been weakened and the people of the nation come to recognize its weakness, the decline is almost inexorable and thus very difficult to stem. The old religion loses both its hold on the minds and hearts of its adherents and also its political and institutional support within the nation. Once that occurs, reform and revitalization become very difficult.

Our data seem to support the conclusion that the process of revitalizing an old majority religion occurs primarily in those nations where the political and institutional support of the majority religion is still very strong and where religious leaders can count on the support of powerful political and ideological leaders.

The Effect of Proselyting Denominations

Secularization theory usually posits the replacement of religion by irreligion. Conversely, one of the most notable features of our data is the typical pattern of replacement of one religion by another. As we have shown elsewhere, in almost every nation in which the Catholic Church is in the majority it is declining while Protestant churches are growing, and vice versa.[23] Likewise, when an indigenous tribal religion declines, it is almost invariably replaced by another religion, often a proselyting Christian denomination.

Secularization theory largely ignores the great efforts by many religions, especially Christian denominations, to proselyte and spread their faith to other people. This process has been markedly successful in Africa, Oceania, and some parts of Asia, and much less successful in Europe. The religious freedom that now exists in Europe, Latin America, North America, and some parts of Africa has encouraged many proselyting denominations to expend great efforts to make inroads for their particular faiths in these areas. This process, perhaps more than secularization, accounts for much of the religious change that has occurred in the nineteenth and twentieth centuries.

At certain stages or places in the cycle of religious transformation, social conditions are favorable to proselyting and conversion. Religious freedom coupled with a decline in the strength of and commitment to an established religion are prime prerequisites for the success of proselyting denominations. The decline of the majority religion itself, of course, needs to be explained; so we are not much further in our explanation of the causes of religious transformation or proselyting success. But from the point of view of the proselyting religion, knowing where to proselyte may be as important as knowing why the nation is such a fertile field.

This suggests that in the cycle of religious transformation there is a "window of opportunity" for the development of new sects or the growth of proselyting denominations.[24] This window of opportunity may last for a considerable number of years, perhaps even decades. Proselyting success may be relatively slow at first as the process of decline of the majority religion begins, but as the weakness of the traditional religion becomes apparent, the success of alternative proselyting denominations will increase. This success will be even more notable as new congregations are established, and the new converts reach out through social relationships to others. Proselyting success is likely to be facilitated both by favorable social conditions and by the newly established social networks of converts to the new religion.

Reform and Renewal

Eight nations could not be placed in one of the six stages. In each one, the majority religion declined from 1900 to 1970 and then grew between 1970 and 1980, although this growth was very limited. This renewal of a majority religion does not fit the cyclical model, but it does fit our view of the complexity and diversity of religious transformation. The processes of growth and decline of religions are not invariant but instead are accompanied by fluctuations of commitment and renewal. While reform and revitalization are often short-term, as they appear to be in these eight nations, they are to be expected in many cases. Because Barrett's data do not allow us to examine religious changes *within* the 1900-to-1970 time period, we can only surmise that such short-term fluctuations in other nations are much more numerous than our data allow us to see.

Five of the eight nations in this category are Muslim nations, and the growth rate between 1970 and 1980 (which reverses the long-term decline) is extremely small for all of them. Thus, we do not consider these data (either the number of such nations or the rate of conversion to the majority religion in these nations) a serious challenge to our model of cyclical religious change. In many ways, these nations are similar socially and religiously to those nations in Stages Three and Four. In fact, the very weak demonstration of resurgence of the majority religion in these nations probably indicates a minor variation in what is likely to be a gradual transition to decline in these nations.

Summary of Research Findings

Among the most significant findings of this study are the following:
Worldwide there are over twice as many nations (72 percent) in which the majority religion has declined since 1900 as there are nations with relative stability (28 percent) of the majority religion.

Folk religion is declining everywhere and is perhaps more subject to decline in numbers of adherents than any other type of religion.

Decline in adherence to the majority religion is presently most prevalent in the Caribbean, Africa, Europe, Oceania, and Latin America.

Christian denominations have declined in influence in many areas of the world; however, Christian denominations are also the most likely to replace another declining religion, especially in Africa.

Stability of the majority religion is most likely to be found in the Middle East, Central Asia, and North Africa. These are areas in which Muslim, Buddhist, and Hindu faiths are most prevalent. The place of religion in the cultural life of a nation, the political clout of religion, and restrictions on proselyting in these nations help to explain the ability of these religions to resist replacement.

Political factors have a great influence on the growth and decline of religions. No comprehensive understanding of religious transformation can be achieved without examining the role of politics in this change. Colonialism has had a great influence in many parts of the world, and Marxist repression of established religion has generated religious change in many others.

The decline in the number of adherents to a majority religion begins slowly and gradually but picks up momentum as the decline continues. Decline often follows an exponential curve.

The processes of social change and modernization influence the decline of a traditional religion much earlier than secularization theory suggests, with many nations at the lowest levels of economic development already experiencing such declines.

Nations just peaking in influence and beginning to decline are more likely to be those at a moderate level of economic development. The peak in number of adherents often tends to be reached at very high levels, usually over 90 percent of the society's population.

All but eight of the two hundred nations fit the cyclical model. These eight nations represent short-term trends toward religious reform after a relatively long period of decline. They are very similar to the nations in Stages Three and Four and can be placed quite comfortably in one of those stages. An infusion of new religious zeal seems to account for the revitalization of the majority religion in these nations.

A "window of opportunity" is available for proselyting denominations in nations experiencing religious decline in the majority religion. Proselyting should result in slow growth as the majority religion begins to decline, then more rapid growth as the decline of the majority religion increases. Proselyting denominations are experiencing the greatest growth in Africa, with lesser growth in Latin America, the Caribbean, and some areas of Asia.

With the exception of six Marxist nations, no nation has a predominance of atheists and/or nonreligious people. The percentage of irreligious people is small even in highly secularized nations in Western Europe. The percentage of atheists and nonreligious people is growing, however, in virtually every nation in the world.

DISCUSSION AND CONCLUSIONS

We began by noting that secularization theorists generally make four assumptions about religious change: secularization, or a decline in the number of believers and in the influence of religion, is linear and inevitable, is due primarily to the condition of modernization, and therefore is found primarily in Western nations.

In contrast, we found that the decline in the strength of a religion is exponential, that religious change is generally cyclical rather than linear, that premodern, non-Western societies are more likely to experience a decline in the number of adherents to the majority religion than modern Western societies, and that processes of reform and revitalization that work against the processes of secularization are present in some societies, although in relatively weak form.

The number of atheistic and nonreligious people has grown in most societies of the world, but they represent only very small percentages in most societies. Where atheists or nonreligious people represent over 10 percent of the population, the society is likely to be a Western industrialized nation or a Marxist nation.

If secularization theory were modified and revised to eliminate the extreme assumptions noted earlier, it could be applied to the decline of the majority religion in many nations during one part of the life cycle of a religion. Although economic change and modernization certainly have an influence on religious change, political factors such as Marxist hegemony, colonialism, religious freedom, and the political clout of an established religion also appear to have great influence on religious change in many nations. Thus, the causes of religious change are much broader than usually envisioned by secularization theory. In Chapter 8 we assess the relative contribution of some political and economic conditions to the religious changes we have noted here.

As a general conclusion, decline in the strength of one religion is usually accompanied by growth in another religion, so growth and decline are complementary rather than competing processes. But religious decline also is accompanied by the growth of irreligion, atheism, and religious inactivity. We may therefore conclude that, on the whole, there is evidence of an overall decline in the strength of religion worldwide as established religions are being replaced by both new religions and nonreligious value orientations.

Religious change is a multifaceted phenomenon that is often more cyclical than linear. It is present in the least-developed nations. It is influenced by a number of social causes, with political factors being among the most significant. Secularization theory, especially those brands based on the "Enlightenment hypothesis," do not explain religious changes very well. It is time to reassess the relatively weak empirical foundations of secularization theory and move on to more empirically based explanations of religious change.[25]

Table 6.6

Appendix: Data on Religious Change for Each Nation in the Study

STAGE ONE: DECLINE (The majority religion in 1900 declined in percentage between 1900 and 1980, but remained the majority religion, for nations with GNP less than $3,500 per year.)

Nation	Majority Religion	Percent in 1900	Percent in 1970	Rate of Decline 1970-1980
American Samoa	Protestant	94.7%	78.4%	-.0070
Andorra	Catholic	99.6	99.1	.0000
Anquilla	Protestant	99.3	97.6	-.0002
Antigua	Protestant	96.0	88.2	-.0018
Argentina	Catholic	97.4	92.5	-.0010
Bahamas	Protestant	87.3	72.6	-.0074
Barbados	Protestant	99.4	89.2	-.0073
Benin	Tribal	91.8	66.6	-.0091
Bermuda	Protestant	78.8	72.6	-.0053
Bolivia	Catholic	93.6	93.2	-.0008
Botswana	Tribal	85.7	56.3	-.0143
Brazil	Catholic	95.3	90.2	-.0031
British Virgin Islands	Protestant	99.6	92.0	-.0108
Cape Verde	Catholic	99.0	97.5	-.0018
Cayman Islands	Protestant	98.9	94.2	-.0009
Chile	Catholic	96.0	84.3	-.0032
China (Taiwan)	Chinese Folk	75.6	51.4	-.0061
Comoros	Muslim	99.9	99.2	-.00001
Cook Islands	Protestant	99.3	86.1	-.0013
Costa Rica	Catholic	98.5	91.0	-.0006

Table 6.6 (continued)

Stage One (continued)

Nation	Majority Religion	Percent in 1900	Percent in 1970	Rate of Decline 1970-1980
Cyprus	Orthodox	77.3	76.3	-.0007
Djibouti	Muslim	99.5	86.7	-.0003
Dominica	Catholic	94.0	89.8	.0000
Dominican Republic	Catholic	97.8	97.2	-.0007
El Salvador	Catholic	98.0	96.8	-.0007
French Guiana	Catholic	92.8	87.6	-.0009
French Polynesia	Protestant	77.2	59.5	-.0111
Gibraltar	Catholic	89.9	78.5	-.0011
Guadeloupe	Catholic	98.9	95.7	-.0007
Guam	Catholic	99.8	79.5	-.0001
Guatemala	Catholic	99.4	95.0	-.0012
Guinea-Bissau	Tribal	81.0	52.2	-.0061
Haiti	Catholic	95.2	84.3	-.0022
Honduras	Catholic	97.0	96.3	-.0006
Hong Kong	Chinese Folk	89.4	52.0	-.0094
India	Hindu	80.0	79.8	-.0007
Isle of Man	Protestant	94.4	82.9	.0000
Jamaica	Protestant	90.9	74.7	-.0047
Jordon	Muslim	94.2	93.7	-.0010
Kuwait	Muslim	99.7	94.6	-.0001
Laos	Buddhist	60.3	57.9	-.0002
Macao	Chinese Folk	82.2	58.8	-.0098
Maldives	Muslim	100.0	99.9	.0000
Martinique	Catholic	99.8	96.4	-.0009
Mexico	Catholic	98.8	96.1	-.0018

Table 6.6 (continued)

Stage One (continued)

Nation	Majority Religion	Percent in 1900	Percent in 1970	Rate of Decline 1970-1980
Montserrat	Protestant	90.0	86.0	-.0023
Mozambique	Tribal	96.4	57.8	-.0193
Nicaragua	Catholic	97.2	95.5	-.0010
Oman	Muslim	100.0	99.0	-.00001
Panama	Catholic	87.0	85.9	-.0012
Portugal	Catholic	99.9	96.6	-.0026
Puerto Rico	Catholic	99.8	92.2	-.0007
Qatar	Muslim	99.6	95.3	-.0007
Romania	Orthodox	91.5	64.2	-.0025
St. Helena	Protestant	100.0	99.1	-.0006
St. Kitts-Nevis	Protestant	94.5	88.5	-.00002
St. Vincent	Protestant	93.9	79.8	-.0041
Samoa	Protestant	90.8	76.3	-.0014
San Marino	Catholic	100.0	95.9	-.0008
Saudi Arabia	Muslim	100.0	99.3	-.0001
Sierra Leone	Tribal	85.4	53.7	-.0047
Somalia	Muslim	99.9	99.7	-.00001
Timor	Tribal	87.6	65.5	-.0104
Togo	Tribal	95.1	56.2	-.0216
United Arab Emirates	Muslim	99.9	95.4	-.0002
Upper Volta	Tribal	90.0	55.4	-.0217
U.S. Virgin Islands	Protestant	80.0	62.2	-.0033
Uraguay	Catholic	61.2	61.0	-.0026
Vietnam	Buddhist	69.3	57.8	-.0063
South Yemen	Muslim	97.5	99.4	-.00004

Table 6.6 (continued)

STAGE TWO: DOMINANCE (For nations with GNP per capita less than $3,500).

Stage Two-A: Displacement (The majority religion in 1900 was displaced by another majority religion by 1970.)

NATION	Majority Religion in 1900	%	Majority Religion in 1970	%	Rate of Chg. 1900 Maj. Rel. 1970-80	Rate of Chg. 1970 Maj. Rel. 1970-80
Albania	Muslim	68.5	Nonrelig.	64.4	-.0296	+.0170
Angola	Tribal	99.4	Catholic	61.4	-.0569	+.0131
Belize	Protestant	54.5	Catholic	64.6	-.0087	+.0040
Burundi	Tribal	99.8	Catholic	67.6	-.0521	+.0179
China	Chinese Folk	79.7	Nonrelig.	64.2	-.0251	+.0032
Congo	Tribal	97.5	Catholic	53.3	-.0322	+.0013
Cuba	Catholic	96.9	Nonrelig.	50.1	-.0223	+.0111
Equatorial Guinea	Tribal	94.6	Catholic	76.3	-.0332	+.0005
Gabon	Tribal	92.5	Catholic	65.0	-.0154	+.0004
Mali	Tribal	69.9	Muslim	78.0	-.0131	+.0031
Mongolia	Shamanist	60.6	Nonrelig.	61.2	-.0132	+.0056
Namibia	Tribal	91.3	Protestant	67.1	-.0356	+.0015
Nauru	Tribal	80.0	Protestant	58.3	.0000	-.0013
Niger	Tribal	54.9	Muslim	86.0	-.0161	+.0026
North Korea	Shamanist	94.2	Nonrelig.	61.0	-.0318	+.0097
Northern Solomons	Tribal	100.0	Catholic	83.6	-.0040	+.0003
Panama Canal Zone	Catholic	53.1	Protestant	62.0	-.0017	-.0011
Papua New Guinea	Tribal	95.9	Protestant	62.0	-.0591	+.0030
Sao Tome & Principe	Tribal	96.9	Catholic	92.2	-.0240	+.0002

Table 6.6 (continued)

Stage Two-A (continued)

NATION	Majority Religion in 1900	%	Majority Religion in 1970	%	Rate of Chg. 1900 Maj. Rel. 1970-80	Rate of Chg. 1970 Maj. Rel. 1970-80
Solomon Islands	Tribal	79.5	Protestant	72.9	-.0186	+.0009
Tonga	Polynesian Indigenous	82.0	Protestant	60.3	-.0290	+.0002
Vanuatu	Tribal	67.8	Protestant	66.7	-.0438	+.0047

Stage Two-B: Ascendance (Several minority religions in 1900 were replaced by one majority religion by 1970.)

NATION	Majority Religion in 1900	%	Majority Religion in 1970	%	Rate of Chg. 1900 Maj. Rel. 1970-80	Rate of Chg. 1970 Maj. Rel. 1970-80
Ethiopia	Tribal Orthodox Muslim	37.1 36.3 26.0	Orthodox	50.3	-.0224	+.0049

Table 6.6 (continued)

Stage Two-C: Supercession (A majority religion in 1900 was replaced by
several minority religions by 1970.)

Nation	Majority Religion in 1900	%	Chief Religions (over 20%) in 1970	%	Yearly Rate of Change 1970-1980
Cameroon	Tribal	94.6%	Tribal	31.9%	-.0356
			Catholic	30.0	+.0185
			Muslim	20.0	+.0108
Central African Republic	Tribal	99.6	Protestant	45.5	+.0111
			Catholic	30.0	+.0015
Chad	Tribal	64.0	Tribal	26.9	-.0168
			Muslim	42.0	+.0054
			Catholic	20.0	+.0055
Fiji	Protestant	81.2	Protestant	41.7	-.0020
			Hindu	40.4	-.00004
Ghana	Tribal	90.3	Tribal	33.2	-.0412
			Protestant	26.7	+.0050
Guyana	Protestant	50.7	Protestant	38.0	-.0090
			Hindu	32.0	+.0022
Ivory Coast	Tribal	94.9	Tribal	49.0	-.0122
			Muslim	22.8	+.0059
Kenya	Tribal	95.8	Tribal	28.1	-.0379
			Catholic	24.0	+.0111
			Protestant	22.9	+.0186
Kiribati	Protestant	55.1	Protestant	49.4	-.0029
			Catholic	48.0	+.0025
South Korea	Shamanist	81.3	Shamanist	38.4	-.0359
Lebanon	Catholic	74.0	Catholic	38.5	-.0006
			Muslim	35.4	-.0016
Lesotho	Tribal	88.9	Catholic	40.4	+.0083
			Protestant	38.5	+.0078
Liberia	Tribal	87.4	Tribal	49.8	-.0143
Madagascar	Tribal	60.3	Tribal	49.2	-.0050
			Catholic	25.1	+.0041
			Protestant	22.9	+.0038

Table 6.6 (continued)

Stage Two-C (continued)

Nation	Majority Religion in 1900	%	Chief Religions (over 20%) in 1970	%	Yearly Rate of Change 1970-1980
Malawi	Tribal	95.2%	Tribal	24.7%	-.0261
			Protestant	31.2	+.0089
			Catholic	25.0	+.0118
Mauritius	Hindu	54.5	Hindu	46.1	-.0011
			Catholic	43.0	-.0006
Micronesia (Pacific Island)	Protestant	50.6	Protestant	49.2	.0000
			Catholic	45.4	+.0005
Nigeria	Tribal	73.0	Protestant	24.8	+.0063
			Muslim	44.0	+.0026
Rwanda	Tribal	99.8	Tribal	29.3	-.0434
			Catholic	47.3	+.0202
South Africa	Tribal	57.0	Non-White Indigenous	20.0	+.0111
			Protestant	48.1	-.0023
Swaziland	Tribal	99.0	Tribal	28.3	-.0297
			Protestant	33.2	+.0136
			African Indigenous	26.9	+.0087
Tanzania	Tribal	90.5	Tribal	31.8	-.0338
			Catholic	23.1	+.0260
			Muslim	31.5	+.0037
Transkei	Tribal	80.1	Tribal	30.7	-.0047
			Protestant	43.0	-.0001
Uganda	Tribal	91.2	Tribal	21.9	-.0508
			Catholic	44.0	+.0014
			Protestant	24.5	+.0163
Zaire	Tribal	98.1	Catholic	46.2	+.0053
			Protestant	27.9	+.0042
Zambia	Tribal	99.7	Tribal	34.2	-.0248
			Protestant	31.2	+.0110
			Catholic	24.2	+.0098
Zimbabwe	Tribal	96.0	Tribal	46.5	-.0156
			Protestant	24.9	+.0068

Table 6.6 (continued)

STAGE THREE: GROWTH

Stage Three-A: Sustained Growth   (The majority religion in 1900 continued to grow until 1980.)

Nation	Dominant Religion	Percent in 1900	Percent in 1970	Rate of Growth 1970-1980
Brunei	Muslim	60.9%	62.2%	.0036
Gambia	Muslim	81.0	84.2	.0007
Greenland	Protestant	90.0	98.3	.0003
Grenada	Catholic	57.4	63.6	.0013
Guinea	Muslim	58.0	68.0	.0017
Iraq	Muslim	89.5	95.3	.00001
Ireland	Catholic	89.6	95.1	.0003
Mauritania	Muslim	97.7	99.3	.00003
Netherlands Antilles	Catholic	80.0	86.9	.0003
Nepal	Hindu	77.0	88.1	.0020
Pakistan	Muslim	82.1	96.8	.00003
Reunion	Catholic	52.0	96.0	.0003
Senegal	Muslim	70.0	90.0	.0013
Spanish North Africa	Catholic	90.0	90.3	.0000
Sudan	Muslim	62.0	71.0	.0034
Venezuela	Catholic	92.9	94.8	.00001

Table 6.6 (continued)

Stage Three-B: Stability Through Competition   (Several minority religions
competed for dominance.)

Nation	Major Religions in 1900	%	Major Religions in 1970	%	Yearly Rate of Change 1970-1980
Indonesia	Tribal	45.6%	New Asian	37.4%	-.0057
	Muslim	40.0	Syncratic		
			Muslim	43.0	+.0011
Malaysia	Muslim	48.8	Muslim	49.5	-.0001
	Chinese	25.0	Chinese	24.9	-.0011
	Folk		Folk		
Surinam	Catholic	25.0	Catholic	24.0	+.0189
	Protestant	21.2	Protestant	26.4	+.0100
	Hindu	26.4	Muslim	21.0	-.0015
Trinidad	Catholic	32.6	Catholic	35.6	+.0007
	Protestant	38.1	Protestant	31.0	-.0036
	Hindu	26.4	Hindu	24.7	+.0026
Yugoslavia	Orthodox	45.9	Orthodox	37.0	-.0068
	Catholic	40.6	Catholic	28.0	-.0075

STAGE FOUR: TRANSITION FROM GROWTH TO DECLINE   (The majority religion
grew between 1900 and 1970, then declined from 1970 to 1980.)

Nation	Majority Religion	Percent 1900	Percent 1970	Rate of Decline 1970-1980
Algeria	Muslim	86.6%	99.1%	-.00004
Bangladesh	Muslim	65.6	82.0	-.00004
Burma	Buddhist	86.7	87.8	-.0009
Colombia	Catholic	79.8	96.7	-.0001
Ecuador	Catholic	87.7	96.7	-.0003
Greece	Orthodox	83.3	97.7	-.0002
Kampuchea	Buddhist	85.5	87.3	-.0003

Table 6.6 (continued)

Stage Four (continued)

Nation	Majority Religion	Percent in 1900	Percent in 1970	Rate of Decline 1970-1980
Libya	Muslim	93.7%	96.9%	-.00001
Malta	Catholic	89.0	97.8	-.0005
Morocco	Muslim	96.4	98.9	-.00003
New Caledonia	Catholic	64.2	72.9	-.0007
Peru	Catholic	94.6	95.5	-.0005
Philippines	Catholic	73.0	85.0	-.0012
Poland	Catholic	78.5	83.0	-.003
St. Lucia	Catholic	82.3	89.5	-.0014
Seychelles	Catholic	83.4	90.0	-.0009
Sikkim	Hindu	64.9	65.6	-.001
Singapore	Chinese Folk	49.5	54.2	-.0007
Sri Lanka	Buddhist	59.2	66.1	-.0007
Syria	Muslim	83.1	89.0	-.0004
Thailand	Buddhist	90.8	92.1	-.00004
Tunisia	Muslim	87.5	99.0	-.00002
Turkey	Muslim	77.3	99.0	-.00001
North Yemen	Muslim	98.5	100.0	-.000004
South Yemen	Muslim	97.5	99.4	-.00004

Table 6.6 (continued)

STAGE FIVE: DECLINE

(The majority religion in 1900 declined in percentage between 1900 and 1970, but remained the majority religion, for nations with GNP greater than $3,500 in 1980.)

Nation	Majority Religion	Percent in 1900	Percent in 1970	Rate of Decline 1970-1980
Andorra	Catholic	99.6%	99.1%	.0000
Australia	Protestant	73.6	61.4	-.0177
Austria	Catholic	91.8	89.2	-.0004
Belgium	Catholic	98.8	91.9	-.0002
Bermuda	Protestant	78.8	72.6	-.0053
Channel Islands	Protestant	88.5	77.3	-.00001
Czechoslovakia	Catholic	90.1	51.6	-.0024
Denmark	Protestant	99.2	96.0	-.0008
Faeroe Islands	Protestant	100.0	99.5	-.00003
Finland	Protestant	98.3	95.0	-.0021
France	Catholic	97.1	80.3	-.0047
East Germany	Protestant	89.5	52.0	-.0174
Guam	Catholic	99.8	79.5	-.0001
Hong Kong	Chinese Folk	89.4	52.0	-.0094
Hungary	Catholic	64.2	54.5	-.0011
Iceland	Protestant	99.8	97.4	-.0009
Italy	Catholic	99.6	90.5	-.0083
Japan	Buddhist	79.6	62.0	-.0042
Liechtenstein	Catholic	97.7	90.1	-.0026
Luxembourg	Catholic	98.5	93.9	-.0009
New Zealand	Protestant	83.8	76.0	-.0077
Norway	Protestant	99.2	98.5	-.0010

Table 6.6 (continued)

Stage Five (continued)

Nation	Majority Religion	Percent in 1900	Percent in 1970	Rate of Decline 1970-1980
Spain	Catholic	100.0	97.6	-.0007
Sweden	Protestant	98.8	72.9	-.0058
United Kingdom	Protestant	90.8	75.0	-.0026
United States	Protestant	70.4	52.4	-.0110
U.S. Virgin Islands	Protestant	80.0	62.2	-.0033

STAGE SIX: DOMINANCE (for nations with GNP per capita greater than $3,500)

Stage Six-A: Displacement (The majority religion in 1900 was displaced by another majority religion by 1970.)

NATION	Majority Religion in 1900	%	Majority Religion in 1970	%	Rate of Chg. 1900 Maj. Rel. 1970-80	Rate of Chg. 1970* Maj. Rel. 1970-80
Israel	Muslim	83.3	Jewish	87.8	-.0008	-.0009
Panama Canal Zone	Catholic	53.1	Protestant	62.0	-.0017	0.0011
U.S.S.R.	Orthodox	72.6	Nonrelig.	52.4	-.0007	-.0005

Stage Six-B: Ascendance (Several minority religions in 1900 were replaced by one majority religion by 1970.)

No Cases

Table 6.6 (continued)

Stage Six-C: Supercession (A majority religion in 1900 was replaced by several minority religions by 1970.)

Nation	Majority Religion in 1900	%	Chief Religions (over 20%) in 1970	%	Yearly Rate of Change 1970-1980
Bulgaria	Orthodox	81.0	Orthodox	26.0	-.0016
			Crypto-Christian	39.5	-.0041
			Nonrelig.	22.4	+.0062
Canada	Protestant	56.7	Catholic	46.2	+.0012
	Catholic	41.2	Protestant	44.1	-.0096
West Germany	Protestant	51.3	Protestant	49.0	-.0017
	Catholic	46.9	Catholic	44.6	-.0002
Netherlands	Protestant	60.9	Protestant	45.8	-.0061
	Catholic	35.4	Catholic	43.0	+.0003
Switzerland	Protestant	57.8	Protestant	47.5	-.0013
	Catholic	40.6	Catholic	49.6	-.0006

REFORM AND REVITALIZATION (Majority religion in 1900 declined between 1900 and 1970, then grew between 1970 and 1980.)

Nation	Majority Religion	Percent in 1900	Percent in 1970	Rate of Growth 1970-1980
Afghanistan	Muslim	99.5	99.3	.00002
Bahrain	Muslim	99.7	95.0	.000005
Bhutan	Buddhist	79.0	68.9	.0012
Egypt	Muslim	81.1	81.0	.0003
Iran	Muslim	98.1	97.8	.000004
Monaco	Catholic	94.8	90.7	.00005
Paraguay	Catholic	96.6	95.6	.0005
Sahara	Muslim	99.3	65.3 99.7(1980)	.0000

7

Religious Politicization among Western European Mass Publics

Martha Abele Mac Iver

Although religion has long been one of the most important variables for explaining political attitudes and actions in Europe, and indeed, continues to be one of the strongest predictors of partisan choice, the process of secularization has led some scholars to predict a waning in religion's political role.[1] As church attendance steadily declines, together with the number of persons who consider religion important to themselves, it is expected that other variables will become more important in explaining electoral choices. Inglehart, for example, has suggested that the cleavage structures of Europe are changing, and that materialist/postmaterialist value orientations will replace religion and class as the basis of political polarization in Europe and elsewhere.[2]

Other recent scholarship has suggested that the traditional association between religiosity and the political right may be declining. Suzanne Berger notes a shift to the left among European clergy and argues that, even though the laity remain on the right, there has been a decline in support for the right among church-going mass publics. Much more pronounced has been the liberalization in attitudes on moral issues among the young who remain religious. Percheron reports that even though children may share their parents' religious values, they hold much more liberal views on issues such as abortion, divorce, and homosexuality.[3]

As some religious individuals shift to the left in their political attitudes and electoral actions, while others remain on the right, the traditional relationship between religion and politics in Europe will grow muddier, and it will become harder to detect a substantial correlation. The studies in Berger's collection suggest, however, that religion may well shape the left-wing commitment of some individuals, as it has shaped the right-wing commitment of others. As Kenneth Wald argues, religious *beliefs* themselves may be as important to consider in understanding political actions as the organizational and subcultural ties that scholars have previously emphasized in relating religion to politics.[4] If religious values influence individuals differently, it appears that simple correlational studies of religiosity and political attitudes may underestimate the role of religion within individual belief systems. If we are to understand the role of religion in determining individual political attitudes, it is essential that we follow the lead of Benson and Williams and begin to investigate the self-conscious linkage between religion and politics in the minds of individuals.[5] Elsewhere I report on such a study of Northern Irish politicians; this study addresses a similar question using mass public survey data.[6]

Rather than measuring the passive impact of denomination, frequency of religious practice, orthodoxy, or affective religiosity on political attitudes, my analysis focuses on "religious politicization"—the existence (or nonexistence) of a conscious link between religious beliefs and political views within the belief system of an individual. This study will present data on the incidence of religious politicization among European mass publics, and then consider the determinants of religious politicization as well as its influence upon individuals' political attitudes and partisan preferences.

The data for this study are taken from *Euro-barometer 19*, one of a series of surveys conducted among mass publics in the ten nations of the European Community. Interviews for this research were conducted in 1983 with a total of 9,790 individuals in the ten nations, selected in either multistage national probability samples or national stratified quota samples. Besides two measures of subjective religiosity, the survey includes the following question: "Do your religious convictions play a role in your political preferences?" In other words, this variable attempts to measure whether the respondent self-consciously links his or her religious beliefs to political attitudes. Though a single, dichotomously scored question such as this is admittedly a very limited measure of this conscious linkage, it represents an important initial step toward understanding the phenomenon of religious politicization.

INCIDENCE OF RELIGIOUS POLITICIZATION

Table 7.1 shows the percentage of respondents in each nation who claim that their religious convictions play a role in their political preferences. Not surprisingly, the highest concentration of these individuals is found in Northern Ireland, a political community where religion is the most salient source of cleavage in the society, and political divisions

Table 7.1
Percent Religiously Politicized in European Community Nations

NATION	ALL	AMONG THE "HIGHLY RELIGIOUS"*
Northern Ireland	29.7%	36.1%
Netherlands	28.3	63.3
Luxembourg	25.0	45.8
Ireland	24.8	30.8
Greece	24.4	31.2
Belgium	22.6	49.0
Italy	20.0	27.2
France	18.3	41.9
Germany	17.3	46.2
Great Britain	13.3	26.2
Denmark	5.9	21.2

* Those scoring 8-10 on a 10-point scale on the question: "To what extent is God important in your life?"

occur almost completely along religious lines. Almost equal proportions of the Dutch respondents, however, also assert that religion influences their political preferences. As might be expected, the percentage of religiously politicized individuals rises dramatically when we consider only the most religious respondents (those scoring 8–10 on a 10-point scale measuring the subjective importance the respondent attaches to God in his or her life). The most dramatic increase occurs in the Netherlands, where over 60 percent of the highly religious are also religiously politicized. This relatively high percentage is undoubtedly related to the traditional "pillarization" of Dutch society, where Calvinist and Catholic parties have played major roles in the political system and have very consciously sought to apply religious principles to politics.[7]

The primary religious identity in the country may help to explain the variation in degree of religious politicization. The group of countries with middle-range proportions of these religiously directed citizens are primarily Roman Catholic in composition (or Eastern Orthodox in the case of Greece), while the countries with the lowest proportions are primarily state-church Protestant (Great Britain and Denmark) or mixed (Germany). Except for the Dutch and the Northern Irish, European Protestants have not developed political parties or as comprehensive a so-

Table 7.2
Pearson Product-Moment Correlations between Religiosity and Religious Politicization for European Community Nations

NATION	CORRELATION
France	.37
Belgium	.42
Netherlands	.52
Germany	.38
Italy	.21
Luxembourg	.33
Denmark	.26
Ireland	.22
Great Britain	.29
Northern Ireland	.19
Greece	.20

ciopolitical doctrine as have Roman Catholics, and it is probable that the higher concentration of religiously directed citizens in Catholic countries is related to this disproportionate attention to political theology.[8]

Individuals in Catholic and mixed countries are also more likely to see God as very important in their lives, and this greater religiosity may also account for the greater degree of religious politicization there. Religiosity is also highly correlated with religious politicization at the individual level, as Table 7.2 indicates. But when we examine only the highly religious individuals, we find that in most countries more than half do not see a direct relationship between their religious and political attitudes (see Table 7.1). It is important to determine which factors distinguish equally religious individuals who differ on this crucial question.

DETERMINANTS OF RELIGIOUS POLITICIZATION

What factors might lead to religious politicization among highly religious individuals? Inglehart's discussion of the transition from social organizational mobilization to cognitive mobilization suggests several hypotheses.[9]

Membership within a church or other religious organization might serve to mobilize or at least politicize an individual through the influence of clergy or activist laity who may communicate institutional views on the relationship between religious beliefs and politics. Denomination might also be an important predictor, with Catholics expected to be more likely than Protestants to be religiously politicized because of the greater attention to sociopolitical issues within the Roman Catholic Church. Because a denomination question was not included in the survey, however, it is not possible to test this hypothesis here.

In contrast to the more traditional organizational mobilization explanations, the theory of cognitive mobilization would suggest that higher levels of education would provide individuals with the skills needed to become politically active. The educational experience would encourage political interest and stimulate individuals to think systematically and critically about how their values relate to the political world. Though religiosity has traditionally been associated with lower levels of political interest,[10] among the highly religious the level of education and political interest may be of considerable importance in explaining whether or not individuals see connections between their religious and political beliefs. Inglehart's theory would predict that cognitive mobilization variables will become more important than organizational mobilization variables (such as church membership) over time.

Because the dependent variable, religious politicization, is dichotomous, a logit model is more appropriate than a more standard least-squares regression model for analyzing how well the independent variables help to explain the phenomenon in question.[11] In the following analysis, a log-linear model is used to fit the logit model, because the independent variables are qualitative and the results can be graphed easily and interpreted intuitively. After preliminary analyses indicated that the demographic variables of age, sex, and class were negligible predictors of religious politicization, they were dropped, and the analysis was conducted using education, political interest, and church or religious organization membership as predictors. Since only the most religious individuals were included in this analysis, religiosity (importance of God to the individual) was not included. The relatively small number of cases indicated that conducting separate analyses for each country was not a viable option; so the results presented here are for Europe as a whole.

In the log-linear logit analysis described below, the dependent variable is technically the natural log of the odds being religiously politicized— or the "log odds." The raw frequency data are presented in tabular form in Table 7.3, with the ratios of religiously politicized to non–religiously politicized (the odds) for each combination of independent variables, together with their natural logarithms, in the last two columns. As is evident from the table, those individuals who are church members with low political interest and low education have nearly "even odds" (.99)

Table 7.3
Religious Politicization by Church Membership, Political Interest, and Education

			REL POL (Freqency)	N-REL POL (Frequency)	ODDS RATIO: REL POL/ N-REL POL	NATURAL LOG OF ODDS RATIO
CHURCH MEMBERS	Hi PI	Hi ED	122	75	1.63	.49
	Hi PI	Lo ED	137	117	1.17	.16
	Lo PI	Hi ED	89	52	1.71	.54
	Lo PI	Lo ED	162	164	.99	-.01
NON MEMBERS	Hi PI	Hi ED	102	177	.58	-.55
	Hi PI	Lo ED	159	442	.36	-1.02
	Lo PI	Hi ED	110	284	.39	-.95
	Lo PI	Lo ED	397	1044	.38	-.97

PI: Political Interest

ED: Education

REL POL: Religiously Politicized

N-REL POL: Non-Religiously Politicized

only highly religious individuals (those scoring 8-10 on a 10 point scale on the question: "To what extent is God important in your life?") were included in this analysis.

of being or not being religiously politicized. Non–church members of all categories have much lower odds of being religiously politicized, while church members with higher education have greater odds.

Table 7.4 presents the results of fitting nine hierarchical log-linear models to the data in Table 7.3. The first model listed is the saturated model, which includes all possible interactions and the main effects of the three independent variables in the analysis. Interaction terms are dropped systematically in each of the subsequent models. The G^2, or likelihood ratio statistic,is used to test the hypothesis that the model is appropriate, or "fits" the observed data.

In the right columns of Table 7.4, the effects of the independent variables and interaction terms are tested by systematically contrasting models including those variables or interactions with models that do not. Likelihood ratio tests were conducted by calculating the difference in G^2 between the contrasted models and determining the significance of that difference. A large difference indicates a substantial loss of fit by excluding a particular variable or interaction, which is then concluded to be significant in explaining the variability of the dependent variable. Differences were significant only for main effects of church membership and education, with the former substantially more important than the latter. The three-way interaction among church membership, political interest, and education is *marginally* significant.

These findings are presented graphically in Figure 7.1. The graphs of the sample logits, or log odds, from Table 7.3 illustrate the overwhelming effect of membership in a church or religious organization upon religious politicization. The other relationships are more complex. Among church members, high education makes it much more likely for an individual to be religiously politicized. This is also true for non–church members with high political interest, but not for non–church members who have low political interest. The complex three-way interaction noted above is evident in the role played by church membership and education in the effect that political interest has on religious politicization. As the graph indicates, high political interest substantially increases the odds of highly educated, non–church members being religiously politicized. Indeed, unless non–church members have both higher education and high levels of political interest, they are extremely unlikely to be religiously politicized. But high political interest is not as important for church members and, indeed, slightly decreases the odds of religious politicization for them.

The results of this analysis indicate the continued importance of organizational membership in politicizing religious individuals. The church or religious organization still plays a major role in leading individuals to see a relationship between their faith and their political positions, though education contributes somewhat too. Contrary to the

Table 7.4
Log-Linear Models Fit to Data in Table 7.3 and Contrasted to Test Logit-Model Parameters

MODEL	DF	G²	PROB	MODELS CONTRASTED	SOURCE	DF	G² DIFF
1 CPE, R	0	0.00	----				
2 CPE, RCE, RPE, RCP	1	3.79	.0517	1 vs 2	Chr Membership x Pol Interest x Education	1	3.79*
3 CPE, RPE, RCE	2	3.79	.1506	2 vs 3	Chr Membership x Pol Interest	1	0.00
4 CPE, RPE, RCP	2	5.20	.0744	2 vs 4	Chr Membership x Education	1	1.41
5 CPE, RCE, RCP	2	5.74	.0568	2 vs 5	Pol Interest x Education	1	1.95
6 CPE, RP, RE, RC	4	7.70	.1031				
7 CPE, RE, RP	5	202.18	.0000	6 vs 7	Chr Membership	1	194.50***
8 CPE, RE, RC	5	8.95	.1111	6 vs 8	Pol Interest	1	1.25
9 CPE, RC, RP	5	19.38	.0016	6 vs 9	Education	1	11.68**

R = Religious Politicization
P = Political Interest

C = Church Membership
E = Education

* $p = .0517$
** $p = <.01$
*** $p = <.0001$

Figure 7.1
Log Odds of Being Religiously Politicized, by Church Membership, Political Interest, and Education

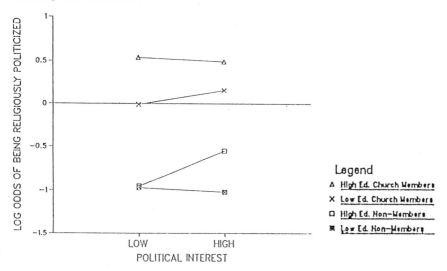

Legend
△ High Ed. Church Members
✕ Low Ed. Church Members
□ High Ed. Non-Members
✕ Low Ed. Non-Members

hypotheses, these data indicate no main effects of political interest, though its effect is marginally significant when it interacts with other predictors.

EFFECTS OF RELIGIOUS POLITICIZATION ON POLITICAL ATTITUDES

Are there any significant differences in attitude between religiously directed and non–religiously directed citizens? Table 7.5 summarizes the differences in the mean left-right self-placement between religiously and non–religiously directed citizens in each country. In every country but Great Britain, the religiously politicized place themselves farther to the right than their non–religiously politicized compatriots. This finding accords with the well-known tendency of religious Europeans to identify with the right of the political spectrum, and one might suspect that the phenomenon is a function of religiosity rather than religious politicization. When one examines only the highly religious subgroup of the sample, however, one finds differences between the means for these groups that remain highly significant. Again, the religiously politicized are significantly more right-wing than the non–religiously politicized, except in Great Britain and Ireland. Since the left-right dimension is not well defined in Ireland, and the difference is not significant in that

Table 7.5
Mean Left-Right Self-Placement for Religiously and Non-Religiously Directed Citizens

	ALL RESPONDENTS			HIGHLY RELIGIOUS RESPONDENTS		
	Mean Non-Rel. Directed	Mean Relig. Directed	T-Test Prob. Value	Mean Non-Rel. Directed	Mean Relig. Directed	T-Test Prob. Value
France	5.03 (706)	5.86 (170)	.00	5.54 (133)	6.18 (103)	.01
Belgium	5.89 (548)	7.19 (176)	.00	6.28 (119)	7.61 (118)	.00
Netherlands	4.93 (667)	6.45 (260)	.00	5.67 (113)	6.84 (185)	.00
Germany	5.25 (739)	6.68 (145)	.00	5.67 (168)	6.82 (129)	.00
Italy	4.45 (669)	5.35 (181)	.00	4.82 (358)	5.53 (144)	.00
Luxembourg	5.27 (193)	6.76 (66)	.00	6.02 (49)	7.56 (41)	.00
Denmark	5.89 (845)	6.61 (54)	.02	6.70 (130)	6.94 (33)	.47
Ireland	6.28 (601)	6.42 (208)	.43	6.62 (367)	6.54 (174)	.68
Great Britain	5.80 (787)	5.73 (124)	.71	6.31 (246)	5.78 (88)	.00
No. Ireland	5.92 (181)	6.68 (85)	.00	5.99 (107)	6.83 (66)	.00
Greece	4.82 (588)	6.08 (180)	.00	5.62 (288)	6.54 (129)	.00

Left-Right Self-Placement is measured on a 10-point scale, with 1 on the far left and 10 on the far right.

Numbers in parentheses represent the number of cases included.

country, we can for the most part ignore the Irish anomaly in our sample.[12] The British anomaly cannot be as quickly dismissed. Many religious individuals in Britain have been active in left-wing causes, such as antinuclear protest movements, and it is possible that it is this sort of religious individual who is most likely to identify himself or herself as religiously politicized.[13] Nevertheless, even though religious individuals have also been active in the peace movement elsewhere in Europe, the effects of this left-wing attachment do not appear in data for other countries. The general trend is for religious politicization to be associated with the right. Even among the very religious segment of the population, ideological differences can be perceived between those who view their religious beliefs as influential in their political preferences and those who do not affirm such an association.

Given the ideological differences between religiously directed and non–religiously directed citizens, one might expect to find significant differences between these groups on various political issues traditionally linked to the left-right spectrum. But the results of analyses using political attitudes toward economic equality, law and order, defense, and environment issues indicated only trivial attitudinal differences between these two types of individuals. An important exception should be noted here, however: religiously directed individuals are significantly more likely than others to express internationalist concerns. This is reflected in attitudes toward the European Community and aid to the Third World.

Individuals who claim that their religious beliefs play a role in their political preferences are significantly more likely than their secular neighbors to demonstrate high support for the EC in France, Belgium, Italy, Great Britain, and Greece (see Table 7.6). When only the highly religious respondents are analyzed, the relationships remain almost as strong in France, Britain, Denmark, and Greece. (Somer's d_{yx} values indicate moderate associations between religious politicization and views on the EC.)

This phenomenon may be due to the strong emphasis in Christian social teaching on the transnational character of the Christian community and the danger of destructive nationalism that divides Christians from one another. These themes are stressed by the philosopher Etienne Gilson, himself very active in the movement for European integration after World War II, who refers back to *"l'unité spirituelle de l'Europe du moyen age,"*[14] and Dante's *De monarchia*, which envisioned not only a unified Europe, but a unified world government as well. Though the papal encyclical *Pacem in Terris* does not refer directly to European integration, it does stress the interdependence of nations and the importance of international organizations such as the United Nations. Fogarty documents how Catholic social thought has shaped the strong support of Christian Democratic parties for European unity, and others note the

Table 7.6
Differences between Religiously and Non-Religiously Directed Citizens on Support for the EC (percentage strongly supporting)

	ALL RESPONDENTS				HIGHLY RELIGIOUS RESPONDENTS			
	Relig. Directed	Non-Rel. Directed	Somer's d_{yx}	(N)	Relig. Directed	Non-Rel. Directed	Somer's d_{yx}	(N)
France	46.7%	28.5%	.22**	(969)	47.3%	29.0%	.19*	(259)
Belgium	46.5	30.9	.19**	(941)	46.9	43.6	.07	(292)
Netherlands	55.8	50.8	.07	(958)	53.1	50.5	.04	(308)
Germany	47.7	47.7	.06**	(986)	46.7	47.6	.06	(330)
Italy	46.5	38.2	.12*	(988)	47.8	40.4	.12	(592)
Luxembourg	53.6	51.7	.04	(276)	54.5	46.2	.09	(96)
Denmark	35.9	24.6	.13	(999)	44.9	31.5	.20	(177)
Ireland	32.2	26.3	.07	(915)	30.2	26.5	.04	(623)
Great Britain	33.6	15.3	.20**	(983)	35.1	17.3	.17*	(360)
Greece	32.4	20.8	.16**	(923)	35.6	25.8	.14	(513)

The Somer's d_{yx} statistic measures the association between the variables in the <u>complete</u> table for each country, which is not reproduced here.

* Chi-square statistic significant at $p = <.05$
** Chi-square statistic significant at $p = <.01$

special role played by the Christian Democrats in creating the EC.[15] At least one biographer argues that Robert Schuman's religious beliefs contributed significantly to his activity on behalf of European unity.[16] The link between Christian social thought and European unity appears to be perceived by individuals who are religiously politicized, and their positive attitudes toward the European Community reflect this influence.

One notable exception to this finding of significantly higher support for the EC among religiously directed citizens is in Northern Ireland, where this group demonstrates significantly *lower* support for the EC than do the non–religiously directed. (The corresponding *oppositional* data for Northern Ireland to those in Table 7.6 are 27.2 percent and 9.6 percent for the religiously and non–religiously directed, respectively, among all respondents [N = 310]; and 31.5 percent and 10.9 percent among the highly religious respondents [N = 202]. The Somer's d_{yx} in each respective case is .12 and .11, both significant at the .01 level. Note, too, in comparison to Table 7.6, the relatively high proportion who remain in the sample in the transition from all respondents to the highly religious.) Although direct comparison between Protestants and Catholics on this issue is not possible (due to the lack of a denomination variable in the data set), it is possible to use vote intention as a surrogate for religious denomination in Northern Ireland. Further analysis reveals that supporters of the Official Unionist Party (which draws its support almost exclusively from the Protestant community) are considerably more opposed to the EC than are others in Northern Ireland. Unionist supporters also tend to be religiously politicized. But Unionist identity does not wholly explain opposition to the EC; non–religiously politicized Unionists are more supportive of the EC than their religiously politicized counterparts.

Why do these politicized Protestant Unionists show such low levels of support for the European Community, in contrast even to individuals in the newest members of the Community where support for the EC has tended to be lower than in the original six member nations? One explanation can be found in the Unionists' perception that EC encouragement of cross-border cooperation is intended to lead to the eventual unification of Northern Ireland and Eire.[17] Since unification is the Unionists' greatest fear, they adamantly oppose anything, be it the EC or the Anglo-Irish agreement of 1985, that they feel might hasten such an outcome.

Religiously politicized Unionists may be even more likely to oppose the EC because they consider it a Roman Catholic-dominated institution. The Reverend Ian Paisley, now a member of the European Parliament himself, made this argument forcefully in his campaign to take Britain out of the EC in 1975, and he even linked the EC to the prophecy of the ten-horned beast in the book of Revelation (before the Community had grown to twelve). Paisley's eschatological rhetoric about "the evil genius of political and economic integration that motivates the Common Market" has influenced many Northern Irish Protestants, and this may well be reflected in the opposition to the EC found in surveys of mass publics there.[18]

Besides their higher level of support for the EC (except in Northern Ireland), religiously directed citizens are also more likely than their non–religiously directed compatriots to support increases in aid to the Third World, as Table 7.7 demonstrates. While this tendency is most marked in Great Britain, there are also relatively large differentials in percentages of respondents supporting increased Third World aid in France, Northern Ireland, Belgium, Ireland, and the Netherlands. The Somer's d_{yx} measure of association remains respectably strong even when religiosity is controlled, and only the most religious (those scoring 8–10 on the importance-of-God scale) are included in the analysis. These findings are consistent with directed individuals should the expectation that religiously directed individuals should express greater compassion for the needy, as their religion prescribes. But these findings contrast with the conclusions of Rokeach, who reported that Americans who value religion highly tend either to be less compassionate on social issues than others (in the case of Protestants), or not to differ significantly in compassion from the nonreligious (in the case of Catholics).[19] The present results suggest that Rokeach's conclusions may be limited by time or space or both.

The globalist concerns expressed by religiously politicized individuals who demonstrate strong support for the European Community and aid to the Third World suggest the possibility that these individuals hold post–materialist value priorities.[20] Yet Inglehart has reported that a high degree of religiosity is associated with materialist values, and that post-materialists are considerably more secular than their materialist counterparts. When one examines the relationship between religious politicization and value priorities, one finds evidence pointing in both directions. In the majority of European countries investigated, the religiously politicized are more likely to be materialists than are those who see no connection between their religion and their politics (see Table 7.8). But in France and Denmark, and to a somewhat smaller extent in Great Britain and Northern Ireland, the religiously directed are *less* likely than their counterparts to be materialists, and this relationship is strengthened (except in Northern Ireland) when religiosity is controlled and only the most religious are examined. (In most of the other cases, the difference between religiously and non–religiously directed citizens is greatly reduced when religiosity is controlled, indicating that the original observed differences may have been due to religiosity rather than religious politicization itself.)

Table 7.7
Differences between Religiously and Non-Religiously Directed Citizens on Aid to the Third World
(percentage supporting increase in aid)

	ALL RESPONDENTS				HIGHLY RELIGIOUS RESPONDENTS			
	Relig. Directed	Non-Rel. Directed	Somer's dyx	(N)	Relig. Directed	Non-Rel. Directed	Somer's dyx	(N)
France	73.3%	56.7%	.17*	(890)	80.9%	54.0%	.27**	(234)
Belgium	55.1	45.7	.09*	(819)	54.9	54.9	.00	(256)
Netherlands	61.4	53.4	.08*	(910)	64.5	46.4	.18**	(289)
Germany	42.9	38.3	.05	(852)	39.6	35.2	.04	(292)
Italy	71.9	68.3	.04	(942)	72.4	69.4	.03	(564)
Luxembourg	68.7	70.4	-.02	(263)	71.4	69.4	.02	(91)
Denmark	57.5	42.6	.15	(841)	64.3	41.1	.23*	(143)
Ireland	77.3	67.9	.09*	(806)	76.7	68.5	.08	(544)
Great Britain	67.7	46.3	.21**	(899)	69.3	48.0	.21**	(332)
No. Ireland	79.8	62.8	.17**	(277)	82.9	63.6	.19**	(180)
Greece	87.8	91.1	-.03	(784)	86.9	89.2	-.02	(409)

*   Chi-square statistic significant at p = <.05
** Chi-square statistic significant at p = <.01

Table 7.8

Differences between Religiously and Non-Religiously Directed Citizens on Value Priorities
(percentage who are materialists)

	ALL RESPONDENTS				HIGHLY RELIGIOUS RESPONDENTS			
	Relig. Directed	Non-Rel. Directed	Somer's d_{yx}	(N)	Relig. Directed	Non-Rel. Directed	Somer's d_{yx}	(N)
France	31.0%	43.1%	-.13*	(974)	30.5%	45.3%	-.14*	(254)
Belgium	53.5	40.6	.13**	(887)	52.2	43.7	.08	(278)
Netherlands	26.5	18.4	.13**	(924)	30.9	26.5	.03	(293)
Germany	39.9	27.1	.16**	(922)	41.7	29.9	.13*	(316)
Italy	55.1	48.7	.06	(975)	58.4	57.6	.01	(586)
Luxembourg	33.8	28.3	.12	(273)	32.6	32.7	.06	(95)
Denmark	19.7	29.9	-.10	(947)	21.9	35.6	-.09*	(168)
Ireland	46.8	43.3	.04	(897)	49.2	48.8	.00	(609)
Great Britain	21.5	27.2	-.08	(954)	23.7	31.6	-.11	(349)
No. Ireland	37.8	41.7	-.05	(296)	40.8	40.2	-.02	(193)
Greece	59.6	44.1	.17**	(898)	61.7	57.9	.05	(496)

* Chi-square statistic significant at p = <.10
** Chi-square statistic significant at p = <.01

The countries in which we find religiously politicized individuals less likely than others to be materialists are among the most secularized (again, with the exception of Northern Ireland), whether measured by mean religiosity score or by percent religiously politicized (refer back to Table 7.1). What should we make of this? Perhaps Britain and France represent the vanguard of the shift to the left Berger notes among the religiously attached. Religiously directed individuals in Britain and France (together with those in Italy) are farther to the left, on average, than those in any other country under consideration, and this leftist orientation may be related to their lower degree of materialism. Perhaps the experience of being religious and politicized in a national context where religion is devalued encourages the expression of postmaterialist values as a means of identifying with secularized individuals in that society. Ardagh notes how cooperation with the Communists during the Resistance influenced politicized French Catholics to place special value and effort on social justice issues.[21] Many of these politicized Catholics were later attracted to the *Parti Socialiste Unifié*, extreme leftist sects, and the ecology movement—organizations embodying postmaterialist values. In Britain, religious individuals have been active in the Campaign for Nuclear Disarmament and the recent protests against deployment of nuclear weapons, movements that have also attracted a considerable number of postmaterialists. The smaller numbers of religiously oriented individuals in these secular societies may be more concentrated on the postmaterialist left, while the religiously motivated peace activists in countries like West Germany and the Netherlands may be outnumbered by the more traditional right-wing materialist Christians.

Although there is some evidence of an association between religious politicization and various political attitudes and values, religious politicization is much more strongly linked to political party preferences than to particular attitudes. A wide ideological gulf separates those individuals who claim that their religious convictions play a role in their political beliefs from those individuals who make no such claim. Religiously directed citizens are much more likely to prefer a party based on Christian values, while non–religiously directed citizens prefer a party "based on a secular doctrine such as socialism or liberalism" (see Table 7.9). Even when religiosity is controlled, the association between religious politicization and party preference remains high.

Differences between religiously directed and non–religiously directed citizens in their willingness to vote for a Socialist or Communist party are also substantial. Not surprisingly, religiously directed citizens are everywhere less likely than their more secular counterparts to say they might vote for a leftist party. But the level of potential support for Socialist parties among the religiously directed is, nevertheless, sur-

Table 7.9

Differences between Religiously and Non-Religiously Directed Citizens on Preference for a Party Based on Christian Values (percentage preferring a party based on Christian values rather than one based on secular political doctrine)

	ALL RESPONDENTS				HIGHLY RELIGIOUS RESPONDENTS			
	Relig. Directed	Non-Rel. Directed	Somer's dyx	(N)	Relig. Directed	Non-Rel. Directed	Somer's dyx	(N)
France	75.9%	32.6%	.43	(654)	86.8%	65.6%	.21	(202)
Belgium	85.6	40.3	.45	(672)	88.1	56.7	.31	(230)
Netherlands	77.9	20.5	.57	(855)	88.3	47.9	.40	(276)
Germany	89.2	56.9	.32	(759)	91.3	75.5	.16	(284)
Italy	84.8	50.2	.35	(811)	92.6	66.5	.26	(494)
Luxembourg	83.6	40.5	.43	(219)	92.5	57.5	.35	(82)
Greece	69.5	35.6	.34	(735)	79.3	58.8	.21	(407)

All differences are significant at $p = <.005$

The survey question was not asked in Denmark, Ireland, Great Britain, or Northern Ireland.

prisingly high. More than half of the religiously directed citizens in France and Greece might vote for Socialists, while more than one third in the Netherlands, Italy, and Luxembourg say it is possible that they would support Socialists. This finding is consistent with Berger's observation that there has been in Western Europe "a shift to the Left of groups who retain deep religious attachments."[22] Potential support for Communist parties among the religiously politicized is much lower, but still more than 16 percent in Italy and 22 percent in Greece (countries with the largest Communist parties in Europe). Though the religiously politicized are significantly more right-wing than their secular counterparts, their support for the left is greater than one might expect.

CONCLUSIONS

This study has broken new ground by examining the self-conscious linkage between religion and politics in the minds of individuals. Important knowledge has been gained about both the determinants of religious politicization and the impact it has on other political attitudes.

When the primary predictor of religious politicization, religiosity, is held constant, the influence of membership in a religious organization becomes predominant, though education plays a secondary role. Perhaps participation in such organizations exposes people not only to the teaching of the clergy, but also to discussions of politics with others, and the chance thereby to think through the implications of their faith for their political positions. Individuals who have had the benefit of higher education may be able to forge those links for themselves, without as much help from religious institutions.

Why should we be concerned with this minority of individuals who consciously relate religion to politics? The results presented here have shown that even though these individuals are not significantly different from others on many types of political attitudes, they diverge markedly in partisan preference. Even when compared to equally religious persons, these religiously politicized individuals are much more likely than the non–religiously politicized to place themselves on the political right (except in Britain), and to prefer Christian Democratic parties over secular (especially Socialist) parties. On the whole, they also have a more internationalist perspective on the world, as evidenced in their greater support for aid to the Third World and for European integration. It is probable that they differ significantly from others in their attitudes on moral issues as well, though the data did not permit a test of this hypothesis here.

Because only a minority (except in the Netherlands) of those preferring a Christian Democratic party consider their political views to be influenced by their religious views, it is unlikely that religious politicization is simply an inference made by individuals from an already existing party preference. Rather, it appears that individuals may have coherent belief systems that account for complex linkages in religious and political beliefs. Of course, this causal question cannot be answered definitively from the cross-sectional analyses presented here. More focused questioning is necessary in future research to uncover the internal dynamics of this relationship in the minds of individuals. Follow-up probes to the question used in the *Euro-barometer* survey, asking the respondents to express what sort of connection they see and how they came to relate their political preferences to their religious beliefs, would be useful in investigating this relationship more fully. Likewise, panel studies following individuals from adolescence into young adulthood and beyond would help to address the causality question more directly.

It is clear, however, that religion has not yet withered away as an important variable in European politics. A substantial minority of Europeans consciously integrate their faith and their politics, or at least see a relationship between the two. As John Stuart Mill observed, such a minority with a belief has a social power far greater than the majority with its mere interests.[23]

8

Protestantism and the Spirit of Democracy

James T. Duke and Barry L. Johnson

Max Weber's thesis that the Protestant ethic was a significant causal factor in producing the industrial revolution and the development of capitalism is well known to social scientists.[1] Although this thesis has been debated widely and is the subject of considerable controversy,[2] there is general agreement that the Protestant ethic had *some* influence on the substantial economic and social changes that have occurred in Western societies over the past several centuries.[3]

This chapter follows Weber's logic and general analysis. It attributes a causal significance to the constellation of values, action patterns, types of social organization, and institutions that accompanied the development of Protestantism. Specifically, we argue that *Protestantism has had a major causal influence in the development of political democracy*, and that democratic political institutions are found more widely in Protestant than in non-Protestant nations.

THEORETICAL BACKGROUND

The connection between Protestantism and democracy has not been explored extensively in the social science literature, although it has been a part of popular discourse for decades. The most direct discussion is by Howard Kainz, who has noted that the conception of God in Christianity is "pre-eminently suited" to democracy:

With regard to the development of a stable and efficient *democracy*, it would seem that a certain mixture or synthesis of all these diverse concepts of God would be at least useful: (1) a conception of the justice and ultimate firmness of God, as conducive to the formation of habits of personal discipline, hard work, and accountability in the democratic citizenry; (2) the idea of God's concern and mercy, as conducive to attitudes of mutual helpfulness and toleration; (3) the idea of God's transcendence, to emphasize the limitations of secular authority, and to assure a higher court of appeal (one's conscience as the voice of God) beyond political spheres; and (4) the notion of the immanence of God in at least a restricted fashion, to assure civil order and sufficient respect for civil authorities. The Judeo-Christian tradition . . . would seem to be pre-eminently suited to maintaining an equilibrium of the above-mentioned values in a democratic society.[4]

Kainz also argues that the "monarchical-aristocratic" tendencies in Catholicism make it "less readily supportive of democratic values than most forms of Protestantism."[5] This argument is consistent with Irving Kristol's, which asserts that Protestantism tends to inculcate in its followers a moral standpoint, including a sense of purpose and moral restraint.[6] This moral stance enables Protestant nations to avoid the pitfalls of both unrestrained capitalism and other authoritarian and aristocratic tendencies.

Michael Novak also notes that liberal Protestants seem to have more democratic values than conservative Protestants, Jews, or Catholics:

The liberal Protestant vision of religion and public policy . . . tends to strive for reasonableness and tolerance, and to be as minimalist as possible regarding differentiation. Liberal Protestants seem to like to stand on common ground. Their tendency is to believe that progress is not likely to be made on those points about which there are serious differences of opinion. Progress depends on cooperation, on broadening the denominator. This attitude is not necessarily shared by those of other faiths. . . . It first makes itself felt when the liberal Protestant appeals to reasonableness and a kind of universality, just where others attach greater values to particularity, to stubbornness. Similarly, where the liberal Protestant tradition is pushing for tolerance and a recognition of commonality, other traditions may sometimes delight in finding the edges of differences. . . . They prefer to state differences clearly and to try to work around them. They take pleasure in the broken points, not the smooth points. . . . Many who are not liberal Protestants emphasize circles of loyalty, clearly defined, which are held intensely. Instead of trying to be minimalist, they feel a strong urge to find and to state those things they want to be loyal to, even if it means breaking off the dialogue a little.[7]

Novak here does not address the issue of democracy directly, yet his implication is clear. Democratic institutions involve compromise and toleration, and those religious traditions that emphasize uniqueness and loyalty tend to be less democratic than the liberal Protestant churches. The causal factor, according to Novak, seems to be a constellation of cultural symbols, beliefs, and norms associated with liberal Protestantism.

Commenting on Max Weber's personal connection with Protestantism, Gianfranco Poggi notes that Weber "came to share an orientation fairly widespread within cultured Protestant circles in the Germany of his youth: the so-called *Kulturprotestantismus*, which proudly asserted if not the verities of Lutheran theology than the West's cultural debt toward Reformed Christianity."[8] According to this view, the culture of Protestantism is responsible not only for the development of capitalism, but also for all the other institutional changes in the West, including the development of democratic political institutions.

S. N. Eisenstadt asserts that what he terms "modern democratic revolutions" occurred primarily in Europe, and were a response to a combination of unique historical conditions, not least of which was Protestantism, which acted as a "solvent" to weaken old institutional structures and enable the development of new structures. Democratic institutions were developed first in pluralistic societies in which "heterodoxy" in both religion and politics was present:

The transformative potentialities of Protestantism were not actualized in John Calvin's Geneva, or John Knox's Scotland, or the Netherlands in the sixteenth and seventeenth century, or early in the colonization of America. In these settings the Protestants enjoyed a political monopoly and were able to impose their totalistic socioreligious orientation. In England, the Netherlands, Switzerland, to a smaller degree Scandinavia, and initially France . . . Protestantism was crucial in transforming European society . . . [and] transcending the traditional setting.[9]

For Eisenstadt, the causal factor is essentially structural: the pluralistic social and religious organization found in Protestant nations.

While Weber was committed to both liberalism and democracy, he also was committed to German nationalism and the place of Germany in world politics, and struggled to reconcile these values. According to Ira Cohen, Weber perceived two universal tendencies in modern societies, both of which worked against democracy. These are inequality and the "organizational [oligarchical] imperative." Thus, "the prospects for substantive democracy do not figure prominently in Weber's conceptual analyses."[10] Put simply, Weber argued that Protestantism was a cause of capitalism but not of democracy.

Marx also did not view capitalism as a causal force leading to democracy. Marx was especially negative toward capitalism, and was critical of the faith held by democratic socialists that democracy could be achieved gradually and peacefully within the framework of a capitalist economy. Marx believed that only through revolution and the creation of economic equality in a communist order would democracy be possible.

Yet it is quite clear that democracy and capitalism grew together in a number of Western European societies. The historical record reveals that democratic political institutions developed within Western nations that were undergoing an economic transformation toward capitalism.

William McCord's discussion of the possible causes of democracy is still one of the most complex and analytical in the literature.[11] He identifies four possible causes of democracy: (1) economic abundance, (2) ideology, (3) self-government, and (4) pluralism. McCord finds merit and problems with each of these explanations. He argues that at the time some European nations became democratic, they were less economically advanced than many Third World nations are today. Furthermore, the nations of Western Europe were not essentially different in economic abundance from their eastern or southern European neighbors. The economic differences between England and Germany, for example, are not sufficient to explain the democratic tendencies of England when contrasted to the authoritarian tendencies of Germany.

Ideological explanations of democracy, according to McCord, center on the following values: antitraditionalism, legitimation of dissent, belief in human reason, and belief in the perfectability of both society and the individual. The weakness of this argument is that it does not explain the failure of Germany—the birthplace of much Protestant and Enlightenment thought—to become democratic in the nineteenth century.

Experience in self-government seems a plausible precondition for democracy; yet McCord notes that Denmark became democratic with a large peasantry inexperienced in self-government. And today, some of the most democratic new nations are those with a long history of only partial self-government under the direction of a colonial power.

McCord finds the most merit in arguments concerning the effect of pluralism on the development of democracy. Nations with many competing social, religious, or ethnic groups are likely to develop political institutions that will compromise vested interests and allow the negotiation of balanced interests. Democratic institutions encourage this compromise and balance most fully. This draws upon the insights of Reisman and Mills,[12] as well as classical liberal political theorists. Historical instances of the effects of pluralism are Denmark, Holland, and Switzerland, all of which went through a process of pluralization before becoming democratic.

Finally, Adam Przeworski argues that all structural or cultural factors act only as facilitating or constraining mechanisms for democracy, and individual human action and unique situational conditions are also extremely important.[13] If we accept this point of view, we should expect that social factors will explain some of the variance in democracy, while a sizeable portion of unexplained variance will remain.

Drawing on the work of these authors, we hypothesize a close connection between Protestantism and democratic political institutions.

If we follow Eisenstadt's logic, we can argue that societies that were
initially pluralistic and democratic, due to nonreligious causes, were
more likely to develop a liberal Protestant tradition. In this case, political
change precedes religious change. This point of view makes use of a
structural argument that a heterogeneous society with a plethora of
religious, ethnic, or other social groups is more likely to develop democratic institutions. The causal direction of this argument, however, is
questionable at best, since in every case of which we are aware, the
introduction of Protestantism preceded the development of democracy,
rather than the reverse. Thus, primarily on historical grounds, we believe
it is not plausible to accept this argument.

The opposite theoretical position follows a more Weberian line. In this
view, the values inculcated in Protestant societies were major causal
factors in the rise of democracy. According to this theory, religion
causally precedes politics. This may be due to: (1) specific theological
themes in Protestantism, (2) the tradition of toleration and compromise
that developed only in Protestant nations, (3) the moral standpoint and
moral purpose inculcated in Protestant believers, (4) the conception of
God and the implications of this conception for authority structures, or
(5) the secularizing tendencies accompanying Protestantism, which support the separation of politics and religion and allow the negotiation of
both political and religious differences.

Alternative explanations for the rise of democracy include: (1) economic development or economic abundance; (2) capitalism; (3) religious,
ethnic, or social pluralism; (4) economic equality; and (5) religious and
value heterodoxy. The first task in the development of this line of research is to demonstrate a correlation between political democracy and
Protestantism. The second task is to identify a number of alternative
explanations for the rise of democracy and examine the relative influence
of Protestantism versus these factors.

This chapter seeks to demonstrate that political democracy is more
characteristic of Protestant than of non-Protestant nations, and that this
is not a spurious result of economic development or pluralism. Our study
focuses on nation-states as the unit of analysis, and makes use of relatively simple measures of religious adherence, political democracy, economic development, and religious pluralism.

MEASUREMENT OF VARIABLES

Since nation-states are the unit of analysis of this study, we need
indicators of the degree of political democracy, economic development,

religious adherence, and religious pluralism for each nation-state of the world.

Political Democracy

We use several different indices to measure democracy. First, the Freedom House study *Freedom in the World 1980* identified three different measures of democracy: (1) political rights, (2) civil liberties, and (3) status of freedom. The first two measures are on an ordinal scale from 1 (democratic) to 7 (nondemocratic). The measure of status of freedom is a tripartite classification derived from the former two measures.[14] We also use Barrett's Political Freedom Index, a ratio scale in which 100 indicates full freedom and 0 indicates lack of freedom.[15] Because the latter provides interval-level measurement, we regard it as more useful than the Freedom House ordinal rankings.

Economic Development

We use a number of indicators of economic development, treating them as separate indicators rather than combining them into a scale and thereby losing some variation. In much of our analysis, however, we use gross national product per capita as our measure. Our data are drawn from the World Bank's *World Development Report* for 1980. The year 1980 is chosen rather than later years because our data for current religious adherence are accurate for only that year.

Using GNP per capita may yield a biased estimate of economic development and/or modernization for a few nations, particularly oil-producing nations. However, it is a more straightforward and easily interpretable measure than a multiple indicator index of modernization for several reasons: First, data on GNP per capita are available for 199 of the 200 nations with populations over 10,000 in 1980. Other indicators of modernization which we looked at are: (1) physicians per population, (2) infant mortality, (3) caloric supply available, (4) percent enrolled in secondary education, (5) percent enrolled in higher education, (6) percent of the labor force engaged in agriculture, (7) percent engaged in industry, (8) percent engaged in services, (9) percent living in urban areas, and (10) life expectancy. For these latter variables, in no case are data available for more than 123 nations. This means that using any of these measures would force us to eliminate at least 76 nations from our analysis. Furthermore, the intercorrelations among these indicators ranged from .21 to .76, with an average of about .50; so they are only moderately correlated with each other.

Lumping all these variables together is most likely to result in an indicator of modernization that adds little to our knowledge while confounding the effects of a number of separate and not highly correlated factors. Looking at the separate influence of these factors, by contrast, yields more insight, as we shall try to demonstrate later in our analysis.

Religious Adherence

Data on the number of adherents to each of the major religious traditions were obtained from Barrett's *World Christian Encyclopedia*.[16] The data used in this study are relatively noncontroversial, because in most cases a substantial majority of the population of any nation-state adhere to the same religion. To examine the time order of the causal connection, we also used Barrett's data on religious adherence in 1900, in order to control for relatively recent political events in which a religion was replaced by another or by ideological atheism (as in Marxist nations). In 1900, there were forty-five nations in which a Protestant denomination was the majority religion.

Religious Pluralism

Religious pluralism is closely related to ethnic and social pluralism, which could not be measured in the present study. Religious pluralism is indicated by the percentage of the population who were adherents to the majority religion in 1900. We reasoned that the time lag between pluralism and the rise of democracy would best be indicated by using data for 1900 rather than the current era. Most nations were religiously homogeneous in 1900, but a sufficient number (fifty-two) were pluralist to give a good test to the theory.

Economic Inequality

As noted previously, Weber argued that economic inequality was a major hindrance to the development of democracy, and we would have liked to have included this variable in our analysis. Both the World Bank and the United Nations report data on income distribution for some nations, but such information is available for only forty-six nations, and the great majority of these are developed nations. Thus the lack of adequate information on economic inequality forbids us to include this variable in our analysis. Theoretically, however, we believe that there is good reason to explore this variable further when adequate data become available.

Table 8.1
Correlations between Indicators of Political Democracy and Modernization for Two Hundred Nations

| Indicators of Modernization | INDICATORS OF POLITICAL DEMOCRACY | | | |
	Political Rights	Civil Liberties	Political Freedom	Freedom Index
GNP per Capita	.37	.41	.33	.39
Infant Mortality	.55	.56	.54	.59
Physician per Population	.35	.39	.31	.35
Available Calories	.35	.37	.36	.41
Elementary Education	.40	.37	.36	.35
Secondary Education	.52	.54	.46	.50
Higher Education	.54	.58	.49	.51
Agricultural Labor	.50	.52	.46	.52
Industrial Labor	.35	.38	.32	.41
Service Labor	.55	.56	.52	.56
Urban Population	.41	.43	.42	.43
Life Expectancy	.54	.55	.53	.58

FINDINGS

Political Democracy and Modernization

A number of years ago, a series of essays in a collection by Almond and Coleman and another essay by S. M. Lipset observed a substantial correlation between economic development and political democracy.[17] Our data, drawn primarily from 1980, demonstrate that this is still true today. Table 8.1 shows the correlations between four indicators of political democracy and eleven indicators of modernization.

Correlations with political democracy are lower for GNP per capita than for the other indicators of modernization. The correlations are especially high for (a) infant mortality, (b) life expectancy, (c) students in secondary and higher education, and (d) percentage of the labor force in service industries. These probably are better indicators of quality of life than the other measures used, which indicates that quality of life and political democracy are substantially correlated. This points out the methodological weakness in using only GNP as an indicator of modernization and/or quality of life. Again, our dilemma is whether to use

Table 8.2

Means of Indicators of Political Democracy, by Majority Religion of the Nation for Two Hundred Nations

Majority Religion	INDICATORS OF POLITICAL DEMOCRACY			
	Freedom Index	Political Freedom	Political Rights	Civil Liberties
Protestant	78.0	1.4	2.6	2.6
Roman Catholic	60.6	1.9	3.8	3.7
Tribal	34.1	2.4	5.2	5.1
Islamic	30.0	2.5	4.9	4.8
Eastern	46.1	2.2	4.4	4.4

NOTE: Freedom Index (100 = Free, 0 = Unfree);
Political Freedom (1 = Free, 3 = Unfree);
Political Rights and Civil Liberties (1=Democratic, 7=Undemocratic).

a relatively poor measure (GNP) available for all nations or stronger measures available for only about 60 percent of the nations in our study. We have chosen to use GNP with some reluctance.

Religion and Political Democracy

Barrett classified the two-hundred nations of the world according to the majority religion in 1980. For the nations of each religious category, we calculated the mean score on four indicators of political democracy. These data are presented in Table 8.2.

A higher percentage of Protestant nations are democratic by all indicators of political democracy. Catholic nations lean toward the democratic side, whereas nations with Islamic and tribal religions are least democratic. Christianity generally, and Protestantism more specifically, seem to be related to political democracy.

As Weber pointed out, the most modern and developed nations of the world generally are Protestant nations. And since political democracy and modernization are correlated, it is therefore incumbent upon us to demonstrate that Protestantism is related to political democracy when the effects of modernization are controlled. In the analysis to follow, we use GNP per capita as the measure of (economic) modernization, which enables us to include more nations in our analysis. We also include the critically important time dimension by looking at the majority religion in 1900. We do this because it is the long-standing religious heritage of

Table 8.3
Percentage of Nations Classified as Free (Democratic), by GNP per Capita and Majority Religion in 1900

MAJORITY RELIGION in 1900	GNP PER CAPITA in 1980				TOTAL PERCENT FREE
	$0-399	$400-999	$1000-3999	$4000+	
Protestant	0% (2)	57% (7)	91% (11)	95% (19)	82%
Catholic	0 (3)	27 (11)	29 (34)	43 (14)	31
Eastern*	0 (9)	100 (2)	0 (1)	100 (1)	23
Islamic	15 (13)	0 (6)	25 (8)	17 (6)	15
Tribal	4 (22)	13 (15)	0 (7)	-- --	7

* Hindu, Buddhist, Confucian, and Shinto

a nation that has the greatest impact on the development of democratic institutions. We therefore control for GNP per capita and investigate the number of democratic or free nations that originate from each religious heritage. These data are reported in Table 8.3.

This table shows very clearly that Protestant nations are more democratic than other nations, even when level of modernization is controlled. Virtually all of the poorest nations are undemocratic, no matter what religious heritage they have had. But above this poorest level, Protestant nations are consistently more democratic than other nations. Although some percentages are admittedly based on small numbers, and therefore may be unreliable, the strong democratic tendency of Protestant nations is easily apparent in these data.

Protestant nations with lower levels of economic development often are or have been colonies of more developed Protestant nations. The (former) colonial power generally has been successful in inculcating democratic institutions and enabling these institutions to be maintained. Nations of other religious heritages have either failed to initiate democratic institutions, or the democratic institutions they have attempted to establish have not weathered the storms surrounding independence.

Although we do not report the data here, it is also apparent from our inspection of the distribution of religious adherents that nations that were formerly British colonies presently have more religious diversity than colonies of other nations, suggesting that part of the reason for the maintenance of democratic institutions is the institutionalization of religious freedom in nations with a British heritage.

Religious Pluralism and Democracy

A crucial causal question is whether initial religious pluralism leads eventually to political democracy, or whether the establishment of democratic political institutions leads eventually to more religious heterogeneity. In order to examine this question, we have prepared Table 8.4, which lists all nations with GNP under $3,500 in 1980, and shows the nation's score on Barrett's Freedom Index. Also shown is the degree of religious pluralism as measured by the percentage of the population who were adherents to the majority religion in 1900. We also include the major nation of influence, which in most cases was a colonial nation. In some cases, however, especially in Latin America, the nation became independent before 1900, but was still influenced by the former colonial nation's culture and religion.

The best test of the influence of religious pluralism on the development of political democracy is found in the five nations that had no majority religion in 1900—and therefore were most pluralistic. Two of these nations (Trinidad, Surinam) are fairly democratic, but the others (Indonesia, Malaysia, Yugoslavia) have not developed democratic political institutions.

The nations that were most democratic by 1980 are Protestant nations, and the degree of religious pluralism has almost no effect on these nations. Neither does the dominant colonial nation seem to affect the development of democracy in these Protestant nations, since virtually all are highly democratic.

Catholic nations, on the other hand, are much less democratic than Protestant nations. The effect of religious pluralism is hard to assess, since there is great variation, and the number of pluralistic nations is small. Catholic nations influenced by Great Britain all seem to be highly democratic, as do nations influenced by France (except Haiti, which became independent in 1804).

Islamic nations are less democratic than Catholic nations—though again it is difficult to conclude that religious pluralism has an influence on the development of democratic institutions, since the variation among pluralistic nations is so great. What *is* notable is that Islamic nations under the influence of the United Kingdom and France are often quite undemocratic. This suggests that it is religious culture itself, and not the colonial policies of a particular nation, that influences the growth of democracy.

REGRESSION ANALYSIS

In an effort to sort out the causal connections between the variables we have been analyzing, we did a regression analysis with the Freedom

Table 8.4
Current Level of Freedom, by Religion in 1900, Level of Pluralism, and Nation of Influence

NATION	INFLUENCE	FREEDOM INDEX	
COMPETITIVE (NO MAJORITY RELIGION)			
Indonesia	Dutch	33	
Surinam	Dutch	83	
Malaysia	British	58	
Trinidad	British	90	
Yugoslavia	Independent	25	(Ave = 57.8)
OVER 90% PROTESTANT IN 1900			
American Samoa	United States	100	
Antigua	British	90	
Barbados	British	90	
Cayman Islands	British	90	
Isle of Man	British	100	
Jamaica	British	75	
Montserrat	British	90	
St. Kitts - Nevis	British	90	
St. Vincent	British	90	
Samoa	Germany & New Zealand	90	
Greenland	Denmark	90	(Ave = 90.4)
BETWEEN 80% AND 89% PROTESTANT IN 1900			
Bahamas	British	90	
Fiji	British	90	(Ave = 90.0)
BETWEEN 70% AND 79% PROTESTANT IN 1900			
French Polynesia	French	90	(Ave = 90.0)
BETWEEN 50% AND 59% PROTESTANT IN 1900			
Belize	British	80	
Guyana	British	67	
Kiribati	British	90	
Pacific Islands	Germany, Japan, USA	100	(Ave = 84.3)

Table 8.4 (continued)

NATION	INFLUENCE	FREEDOM INDEX	
OVER 90% CATHOLIC IN 1900			
Argentina	Spain	17	
Bolivia	Spain	33	
Chile	Spain	17	
Costa Rica	Spain	100	
Cuba	Spain	8	
Dominican Republic	Spain	67	
El Salvador	Spain	67	
Guatemala	Spain	50	
Honduras	Spain	42	
Mexico	Spain	50	
Nicaragua	Spain	33	
Paraguay	Spain	25	
Peru	Spain	33	
Sp. North Africa	Spain	80	
Venezuela	Spain	92	
Brazil	Portugal	42	
Cape Verde	Portugal	20	
Dominica	British	90	
French Guiana	France	90	
Haiti	France (Independent)	8	
Guadeloupe	France	90	
Lebanon	France	50	
Martinique	France	90	
Puerto Rico	U.S.A.	95	
Portugal	Independent	83	
San Marino	Independent	90	(Ave = 56.2)
BETWEEN 80% AND 89% CATHOLIC IN 1900			
Panama	Spain	25	
Ecuador	Spain	33	
Gibraltar	British	90	
Malta	British	80	
St. Lucia	British	90	
Seychelles	British	70	
Netherlands Antilles	Dutch	90	(Ave = 68.3)
BETWEEN 70% AND 79% CATHOLIC IN 1900			
Colombia	Spain	75	
Philippines	U.S.A.	33	
Poland	Independent	25	(Ave = 44.3)
BETWEEN 60% AND 69% CATHOLIC IN 1900			
Uruguay	Spain	17	
New Caledonia	France	90	(Ave = 53.5)
BETWEEN 50% AND 59% CATHOLIC IN 1900			
Grenada	British	90	
Reunion	France	90	
Panama Canal Zone	U.S.A.	80	(Ave = 86.7)

Table 8.4 (continued)

NATION	INFLUENCE	FREEDOM INDEX	
OVER 90% ISLAMIC IN 1900			
Afghanistan	British	8	
Bahrain	British	33	
Jordan	British	17	
Kuwait	British	33	
Maldives	British	70	
Qatar	British	33	
United Arab Emirates	British	33	
South Yemen	British	0	
Saudi Arabia	British & Independent	17	
Somalia	British & Italian	0	
Comoros	France	20	
Djibouti	France	30	
Mayotte	France	80	
Mauritania	France	17	
Morocco	France & Spain	58	
Sahara	Spain	10	
Libya	Italy	8	
North Yemen	Turkey	25	
Iran	Independent	25	
Oman	Independent	20	(Ave = 26.8)
BETWEEN 80% AND 89% ISLAMIC IN 1900			
Gambia	British	83	
Egypt	British	42	
Israel	British	75	
Pakistan	British	33	
Algeria	France	17	
Syria	France	25	
Tunisia	France	25	
Iraq	Independent	0	(Ave = 37.5)
BETWEEN 70% AND 79% ISLAMIC IN 1900			
Senegal	France	50	
Turkey	Independent	75	(Ave = 62.5)
BETWEEN 60% AND 69% ISLAMIC IN 1900			
Bangladesh	British	33	
Brunei	British	50	
Sudan	British	25	
Albania	Turkey	0	(Ave = 27.0)
BETWEEN 50% AND 59% ISLAMIC IN 1900			
Guinea	France	0	(Ave = 0.0)

Table 8.5

Stepwise Multiple Regression Analysis with Democracy (Freedom Index) as the Dependent Variable

INDEPENDENT VARIABLE	MULT R	MULT R^2	R^2 CHANGE	BETA	SIGNIF.
PROT1900	.524	.275	.2747	.524	.0000
GNP	.573	.328	.0538	.244	.0002
PLUR1900	.573	.329	.0002	.012	.8472

Index as the indicator of democracy, and the following independent variables: (1) GNP (GNP per capita in 1980), (2) PROT1900 (Protestantism as the dominant religion in 1900, treated as a dummy variable), and PLUR1900 (pluralism in 1900, a dummy variable with the dominant religion having less than 80 percent of the population scored as 1). The results of the regression are reported in Table 8.5.

The first independent variable in the regression is PROT1900, which explains over 27 percent of the variance in the Freedom Index. This substantiates the argument made in this chapter that nations having a Protestant religious heritage are more likely to be democratic. The second variable entered was GNP, which added 5.4 percent explained variance. This corroborates research over a long period of time that attributes a causal connection between economic development and democracy. PROT1900 and GNP together explained 32.8 percent of the variance in the Freedom Index, our indicator of democracy.

We also experimented with using measures of quality of life as indicators of development, such as infant mortality. Infant mortality explained considerably more variance than did GNP, but since we did not have data on infant mortality for about eighty nations, we regard this as less accurate than using GNP for more nations. In the future, we recommend efforts to obtain infant mortality rates for all two-hundred nations. Regressions based on such figures, we hypothesize, will yield much higher explained variance than using GNP alone.

PLUR1900 was not statistically significant, and added only 0.02 percent explained variance. Contrary to the arguments of Eisenstadt, McCord, and others, a religiously pluralistic society is no more likely to become democratic than a religiously homogeneous society.

CONCLUSION

The dominant religion in a nation has a powerful impact on the political culture of that nation, and Protestantism has a powerful effect on the development of democracy. Protestantism has a stronger causal connection with democracy than does the level of economic development. And religious pluralism (and by implication social or ethnic pluralism) has no effect on the development of democratic political institutions.

We also tentatively conclude that while Great Britain and France have had a democratizing influence on their Protestant and Catholic colonies, they have had much less influence on their Muslim colonies—suggesting again the importance of religion rather than the influence of a specific colonial nation.

We conclude, therefore, that some causal factors are present in Protestant nations that enable them to establish and maintain democratic political institutions more effectively than nations with other majority religions. We have taken only a first step in specifying these variables—largely cultural rather than structural—associated with Protestantism, and have no adequate measure of them at present. Further work on measurement and specific historical and comparative analyses are now needed to elucidate this process.

Losing Faith in the "Religion" of Secularization: Worldwide Religious Resurgence and the Definition of Religion

William H. Swatos, Jr.

It has become increasingly fashionable in American sociology of religion to be critical of secularization theory. Perhaps the clearest, most comprehensive, and trenchant analysis thus far of the weaknesses of secularization theory—both in its genesis and its predicted outcomes—is Jeffrey Hadden's 1986 presidential address to the Southern Sociological Society. The core of his argument is that in and from its genesis secularization constituted a *"doctrine* more than a theory" based on "presuppositions that . . . represent a taken-for-granted *ideology"* of social science "rather than a systematic set of interrelated propositions"; over time in social scientific circles (which continued to widen in their influence), *"the idea of secularization became sacralized,"* that is, a belief system accepted "on faith."[1] This flank of Hadden's assault, as a matter of fact, was presaged in a series of pieces by Roland Robertson beginning as early as 1971.[2]

The second thrust of Hadden's attack is a fourfold challenge: (1) Secularization theory is internally weak in its logical structure—"a hodgepodge of loosely employed ideas"—first so revealed, indeed, by Larry Shiner as early as 1967.[3] (2) Such secularization *theory* as does exist is unsupported by data after more than twenty years of research. (3) New religious movements have appeared and persisted in the most supposedly secularized societies. And finally, most important for this book, (4) religion has emerged as a vital force in the world political order around the globe. Hadden concludes this thrust with a series of forecasts of the place of religion in society and in sociology for the next fifty years. It is from the last of these that I want to begin. Hadden writes that we should "return once more to the past to see the future. Max Weber's search for

clues about the place of religion in human society took him deeply into
the study of the world's major religions. The future will take us back to
where Weber began."[4]

THE "RELIGION" OF SECULARIZATION

Max Weber's decision at the outset of his sociology of religion not to
define "religion" is well known.[5] So, too, is the definition of Emile
Durkheim, preeminently as it was refabricated at the hands of Talcott
Parsons and his school. Central to the Parsonian thrust was the inte-
grationist or solidarity theme within the Durkheimian formulation; that
is, that religion *unites all those who adhere to it into a single moral community.*
Religion was the glue of society, the source of social solidarity. So
strongly believed was this proposition among social scientists that, in
cases where it was manifestly clear that what participants in the action
system termed "religion" did not integrate the social system, sociologists
nevertheless proceeded undaunted to search out the "real" religion of
society—its latent source of solidarity—and proclaim this as sacred rite
and ceremony. This approach enjoyed great success in the sociology of
religion when applied in monopolistic settings (e.g., Marxist regimes)
but encountered problems with pluralism. The best effort to articulate
such a "religion" for modern American society, for example, Robert
Bellah's seminal essay on "civil religion," has failed to generate an integrated theoretical structure for the explanation of subsequent developments in either American or global systems.[6]

What is wrong with this approach to religion? There are, first, a number of problems inherent in Durkheim's work itself. W. G. Runciman
has summarized three of these, the most telling of which is that Durkheim's "explanation" of religious beliefs in a this-worldly terminus (i.e.,
society) does not actually "explain" them at all; "why, after all, is the
worship of society any more readily explicable than the worship of
gods?"[7] Intimately connected with this "explanation," however, is Durkheim's search for the source of social solidarity, and behind this is his
presumption of solidarity. Although Durkheim is generally cited for "abol-
ishing the role of individual judgment and subjective meaningfulness
of social reality in his theory,"[8] in the concept of solidarity he reintroduces in two types (mechanical and organic solidarity) sociological
"sticky stuff," that is *not* in fact structural but psychoemotional, though
collective rather than individual.

Compounding these problems within Durkheim's theory is the problem of the translation of the title of Durkheim's central text in the sociology of religion into English as *The Elementary Forms of the Religious
Life*. The difficulty here is with the term *élémentaire*, a word that has a
double connotation in French, but in English can be rendered as either

"elementary" or "elemental." Joseph Ward Swain, the translator, chose the former. In so doing he gave a particularly *evolutionary* twist to Durkheim's work that was, indeed, there in the original, but was also balanced there by the sense of "elemental," and this latter was far more the crucial contribution of Durkheim's research—namely, a study of "what pertains to or is one of the constituent parts or basic components . . . of humanity's religious life." Admittedly, Durkheim "did not wrestle with the fact that modern 'primitives' have just as many years of history behind them as do the rest of us to-day," but the use of "the *elementary* forms of religious life, in the sense of an early stage of development," was not the central thrust of Durkheim's work. The choice of "elementary" over "elemental" reflects "the far from insignificant fact that the translation was made at a phase in Western cultural evolution when sophisticated secular intellectuals tended to hold that chronologically early and in its wake present-day tribal religious life was closer, or more manageably close, to the truth about religion generically than our more developed forms."[9] In short, "elementary" was more consistent with the incipient *doctrine of secularization* than was "elemental." Rather than a paradigm study of religion, *The Elementary Forms* became a doctrinaire statement about religion.

That this is more than a semantic exercise may be seen quite clearly when we turn to Talcott Parsons's work as the major hermeneutic on Durkheim in Western sociology for over a quarter of a century, for Parsons increasingly employed an evolutionary approach in his work over the years. Where did Parsons begin his evolutionary scheme but with Durkheim's (and others') descriptions of the Australian Murngin—a *contemporary* people? As his work develops, he adds other contemporary accounts of "contemporary peoples, distributed over the earth's surface . . . rearranged to form a general *historical sequence* of societal evolution," while admitting that he is "able to say little about the detailed sequence of events in the course of which primitive societies begin their differentiation into more stratified societies."[10] The point, however, that is easily lost in such an analysis is that it is for all practical purposes *completely ahistorical*. The Parsonian evolutionary scheme is not based upon a study of religious history but the more-or-less contemporary religious lives of peoples throughout the world whose evolutionary "stage" has been determined by some a priori definition of development.[11] "Secularization" feeds into this evolutionary structure as a "modern" entailment of general developmental tendencies—although Parsons saw secularization far more positively than many subsequent secularization theorists.

Hadden quotes C. Wright Mills's succinct critical summary of Parsons's theory: "Once the world was filled with the sacred—in thought, practice, and institutional form. After the Reformation and the Renais-

sance, the forces of modernization swept across the globe and secularization, a corollary historical process, loosened the dominance of the
sacred. In due course, the sacred shall disappear altogether except, possibly, in the private realm."[12] Although this statement implies historical
description, it is in fact based on *almost no historical evidence*. Rather than
systematic studies of the *past*, it draws from commonsense generalizations about history related to systematic studies of the present.

I am no longer prepared to accept the underlying belief system of
secularization theory—that sometime, someplace in the past there was
a solidary age of faith in which "the world was filled with the sacred."
I base this on increasing studies of popular religion—what it was and
what it was not[13]—as well as some admittedly intuitive skepticism about
constructs we take for granted. For example, the medieval period is
often referred to as an "age of faith," and the monastic communities of
the period are adduced as evidence for this designation. At the same
time, however, we discuss the monastic view of other-worldly asceticism
as a *withdrawal* from the *world*. If the world was so full of the sacred,
why did people withdraw from it in such numbers? My suggestion is
that it was a very secular world, not very "religious," and that this
secular world—which more and more came to display what Agnes Heller
has termed "practical atheism"—slowly penetrated monastic foundations until it was hard in many cases to distinguish between the two,
at which time the Reformation constituted a renewed demand for sac-
rality in all relationships—which, of course, was then itself undermined
in due time. Not clear either is the derivation of much scientific, medical,
and agricultural history from the monasteries: Whence this interest, if
these foundations were so unworldly? Monasteries also preserved not
only "sacred" but secular texts as well. John Paterson writes in his history
of St. Brigid's Cathedral foundation at Kildare that "a scriptorium for
the production of written books seems to have become active" as early
as the seventh century, and "this would suggest that the monastery had
. . . become involved in secular affairs."[14]

What I am willing to accept instead, then, is that over time our epistemologies have changed, that our ideas of "the ways the world works"
have changed,[15] and that these have entailed corresponding shifts of
emphasis in global explanatory structures or bases upon which we at-
tribute credibility or truth. The medieval world view, the Renaissance,
the Enlightenment, and the era of modern science represent such alternative epistemologies. When we consider the relatively short history of
the modern scientific world view, it is not surprising that its episte-
mology has not fully jelled.

THE RELIGION OF DURKHEIM

This returns us to the Durkheimian project itself, what his supposed
definition means, and how it fits into a larger theoretical structure. When

put into a historically developmental perspective rather than a functionalist-evolutionary perspective, the Durkheimian approach becomes at once more limited and more valuable.

First, Durkheim eschewed simplistic evolutionism. He wrote that "humanity is in fact involved in an interminable process of evolution, disintegration and reconstruction,"[16] and it is on this basis that he can argue that "every morality has its own rationality"[17]—a very Weberian phrase, but one that, ironically, does not fit the Parsonian Weber-Durkheim convergence thesis. To talk about "religious evolution," then, on the basis of some unilinear evolutionary pattern is fundamentally un-Durkheimian (as it is un-Weberian).

Second, *The Elementary Forms* was a spin-off from Durkheim's larger "sociology of morals" program—a project almost completely ignored by Parsons, as he attempted to create a value-free sociology into which such a program would not fit. As Robert Hall demonstrates, *The Elementary Forms* is preeminently a study in the sociology of knowledge asserting "that the categories of human knowledge are social creations and that the social determinants and social functions of religion are its important elements"—both rather radical thoughts in Durkheim's own day, when the categories of human knowledge were often argued to be eternal, but religion was frequently derided by the intellectual precursors of much social science as a form of delusion, illusion, or both. Seen in this light, Durkheim's work becomes "a paradigm for the sociological study of religion and knowledge," rather than a definitive statement of the immutable character of religion at all times and places:

Durkheim discovered in the collective religious experience of the Australian primitives the kind of social ferment that he thought was responsible for the generation of collective moral beliefs. What Durkheim's study of religion adds to his earlier work is a description of the social origins of the ideal element in the moral life and an emphatic recognition of the importance of this collectively generated symbolic realm for social order.[18]

To attach more significance to *The Elementary Forms* or to break it off entirely from the core of Durkheim's project—the sociology of morals— at once dishonors Durkheim's credibility as a social scientist and turns his empirical work into an abstract statement of unproved and unprovable doctrine.

A NEW "RELIGION" FOR SOCIOLOGY

Where, then, do we go from here? Early in my own work I considered secularization theory a viable explanation for change in religious systems of action. Yet my own work also carried the suggestion of a problem that I am now convinced "secularization" cannot overcome. I reacted

to David Martin's urging that we erase "secularization" from the sociological dictionary,[19] by saying that if we were to do so, then "we should
do the same to religion/religious."[20] In a sense, this is precisely what
now seems necessary—at least the definition we now have must go.
Sociology needs a new approach to the phenomenon we call "religion."
Three elements are involved in this:

First, we must utterly destroy any a priori association between the
concept of religion and that of social solidarity. As Calvin Redekop noted
over twenty years ago, "the integrating power in society of religion" is
not a social fact, but a largely unsubstantiated social-anthropological
belief.[21] Not only is the very notion of solidarity as definitive of society
suspect, as the Beyer-Luhmann analysis argues, but even if we do accept
some concept of solidarity into our theoretical arsenal, there is no reason
to presume an integrated wholeness that certainly is now difficult to
see, and may well never have existed. We might have a richer theoretical
product if we worked instead from Adorno's aphorism, "The whole is
the untrue."[22]

Second, we must take an approach to religion that permits the construction of definitions that have a relatively high degree of isomorph-
ism with what participants in the action system "know" in the social-
construction-of-reality sense to be religion in their own sociocultural
worlds.[23] I have termed this "situationalism," and it is essentially similar
to the "action theory of religion" of Wallis and Bruce.[24]

Situationalism is not without its critics. William Sims Bainbridge, for
example, has scored the Wallis and Bruce book for its lack of "well-
developed theory," as well as its failure to transcend individual actors
to the collective level.[25] In one sense such a criticism merely represents
differences in conceptions of theory. As George Homans once noted,
every explanation is a theory; what we want are explanations that explain
predictively.[26] Whether these come through formal theory that can be
stated in mathematical terms or interpretive theory that uses meta-
phorical ordinary language really matters little, if they enable us to go
on in an explanatory structure to make accurate predictions.

Situationalism both does and does not do this. When we say that "a
situation is what it is defined to be by participants in the action system"
or "an act that is perceived as real is real in its consequences," we are
making strong predictions at a high level of generality but at the same
time requiring close attention to specifics before any credible predictions
can be offered. We also claim that collective action is always the action
of collected actors. One simply cannot have "collective action" without
specific "individual" actors. This is not psychological reductionism but
plain common sense. "Whatever Durkheim may have said, the people
we study are *not* robots. . . . Excessive preoccupation with so-called theoretical models," I. M. Lewis rightly notes, may conceal a "lack of orig-

inality and the contrasting richness of the peoples we study." If this should be the case, "it is *we*, not *they*, who are the puppets."[27] On the other hand, how individual actors turn into a collectivity remains an important lacuna for situationalism or any action sociology. Situationalism thus must be integrated into a field theoretical approach that combines the admittedly complex ingredients of personality, culture, and social structure, recognizing the possibilities for variation within a range whose limits may be capable of articulation in mathematical terms but whose observed incidence will always be somewhat indeterminant. To argue otherwise is to substitute theorizing for theory, abstraction for explanation, mathematical precision for useful prediction.

What the situationalist perspective requires, in particular, is attention to process, to place and persons across time, and to meanings in action systems, without ignoring the fact that such processes always take place in structures, which may on any given occasion be far easier than processes to specify in a formal calculus. The danger, however, is to reify structure to the extent that it becomes perceived as existing "outside" of process. Both "secularization" and "religion" in much sociological discussion continue to reflect an illogical precedence of structure over process, which begins from a definition of religion that, although internally consistent and elegantly simple, has little demonstrated relationship to the lived experience of persons over time. It is not our task to define religion sociologically but to observe and explain how and why people think and act religiously. This is the point of Weber's "nondefinition."

Third and finally, we must give far more attention to the role of structures of knowledge in our accounts of change and of the relationship between religion and society. Religions at once both provide and reflect epistemologies. They are, as Berger and Luckmann would put it, "second order objectivations of meaning" that both reflect and articulate meaning structures for experience into a larger whole.[28] "Secularization," to the extent that we can treat it as a coherent phenomenon at all, represents a paradigm shift of major proportions in ways of knowing how the world works, in which heretofore widely accepted epistemological assumptions are directly challenged by new experiences. At the same time, it is becoming increasingly clear that at least one of the dominant alternative paradigms—positivistic scientism—cannot account for all that humans experience. Thus we continue to have a creative ferment and a persistence of religion on the part of social actors—both individually and collectively—even in the midst of enormous change. We will in all likelihood continue to see competing epistemological systems for coming generations. What creates a tension in modernity that was not as easily present in earlier eras is that media of mass communications bring competing epistemologies—and with them alternate systems of action (moralities)—immediately into interaction, confrontation, and competition with each other, and this, in turn, cannot be divorced from resource allocation, to which there are obvious limits. "Many individuals in today's culture have reached a state of *cognitive overload*— they simply are no longer able to assimilate and evaluate the multiplicity of various descriptions of reality which face them."[29] The worldwide religious resurgence, with its political dimensions and agendas, represents one attempt to cope with this condition.

Notes

CHAPTER 1

1. The most well-known and articulate expositor of this point of view has been Bryan Wilson (*see*, e.g., Wilson, 1976).

2. Robertson and Chirico, 1985: 219 (textual corrections by the present editor).

3. Robertson and Chirico, 1985: 234.

4. Robertson and Chirico, 1985: 235–37 (textual corrections by the present editor).

5. Robertson and Chirico, 1985: 238–39.

6. Robertson and Chirico, 1985: 238.

7. Skocpol, 1979.

8. There are scores of studies of this kind. Three recent collections are Beckford (1986), Fu and Spiegler (1987), and Hadden and Shupe (1986). The best attempt at the kind of global study I have in mind—though without including the religious variable—is Nielsson's global taxonomy of states and "nation-groups" (1985).

9. Honigsheim, 1968.

10. For Northern Ireland, *see* Wallis, Bruce, and Taylor, 1986; for the United States, *see* the many news analyses that followed Pat Robertson's favorable showing in the Iowa caucuses.

CHAPTER 2

1. *See* Janos, 1986.

2. The sociological use of the concept "world-system" was pioneered by Immanuel Wallerstein (1974), but it has by now taken on a useful existence beyond the specific context of Wallerstein's analyses.

3. Robertson and Chirico, 1985.

4. Tilly, 1985.
5. *See* Robertson, 1983; Robertson and Chirico, 1985; Robertson and Lechner, 1985.
6. Parsons, 1937.
7. Alexander, 1981–84.
8. For an overview, among a large number of critiques, *see* Chirot and Hall (1982).
9. Parsons, 1937.
10. Bergesen, 1980.
11. Alexander, 1981–84; Münch, 1982.
12. *See* Parsons, 1937.
13. Modelski, 1978, 1983.
14. Zolberg, 1981.
15. Zolberg, 1983.
16. Meyer and Hannan, 1979; Meyer, 1980; Boli-Bennett, 1979, 1980.
17. Wuthnow, 1980, 1983.
18. *See* Cassese, 1986.
19. Boli-Bennett, 1979.
20. It remains to be seen whether the recent developments in the European community will alter the fundamental facts of societal existence.
21. *See* Nettl and Robertson, 1968.
22. Marshall, 1977.
23. *See* Nelson, 1973.
24. *See* Robertson, 1983.
25. Lechner, 1985.
26. Wallerstein, 1983.
27. *See* Wuthnow (1980, 1983) for pioneering work in this area.
28. Münch, 1982.
29. Wallerstein, 1982.
30. Note that global cultural pluralism is emphasized in different contributions to world-system analysis. For Wallerstein, the existence of multiple cultures is part of the very definition of the world-system; more recently, he has gone so far as to argue that global movements increasingly draw their strength not so much from the "economic squeeze" itself, but rather from the coexistence of multiple civilizations (1982: 36). How these multiple cultures operate in one global culture, and how they are related to other features of the world-system, remains unclear. In Wuthnow's (1983) theory of cultural crises in the world-system, different phases in the development of the world-economy are associated with various cultural responses—all of which turn out to further cultural diversification. Though the emphasis on diversification is important, the criteria for distinguishing between periods of change and consequences of cultural movements remain unclear. Finally, in his work on globalization Robertson (1983, 1985; Robertson and Chirico, 1985) emphasizes, on the one hand, the crystallization of common cultural concerns, such as "humanity," and on the other hand, the relativization of societies and religions in the new global context, new conflicts centering on distinctly global themes, and the likelihood of varying forms of world rejection. While setting the stage for further work on globalization, these ideas remain primarily "cultural" analyses of the world-system;

their relationship to processes of institutionalization and collective action remains to be spelled out. Nevertheless, it is clear that for the major contributors to world-system analysis global cultural pluralism is a constitutive feature of the world-system itself.

31. *See* Swatos, 1979.
32. Lechner, 1985.
33. Ibid.
34. A. Smith, 1981, 1983; Lechner, 1984.
35. Bull, 1987.
36. *See* Voll, 1982; Esposito, 1984.
37. Wuthnow, 1980, 1983.
38. I would like to acknowledge the important role Roland Robertson has played in the development of many of the arguments in this chapter. I would also like to thank Terry Boswell and John Meyer for their helpful comments on an earlier version of this chapter.

CHAPTER 3

1. Robertson and Chirico, 1985.
2. Simpson, 1987.
3. *See* Hadden and Shupe, 1986.
4. Lechner, 1985.
5. *See* Swanson, 1967.
6. Robertson and Chirico, 1985.
7. Calvin, 1960 [1559]: 35 (emphasis added).
8. Luckmann, 1967.
9. *See* Glassman, Swatos, and Rosen, 1987.
10. Meyer et al., 1985.
11. Wallerstein, 1974.
12. Aron, 1966.
13. Poggi, 1983: 72.
14. Ibid., 73.
15. Hofstadter, 1979.
16. Mead, 1934.
17. Stark and Bainbridge, 1985.

CHAPTER 4

1. *See* Bergesen, 1980, 1983; Robertson, 1985; Robertson and Chirico, 1985; Wallerstein, 1974; Wuthnow, 1978.
2. *See* Luhmann, 1982a: 73–74.
3. *See* Luhmann, 1975: 51–71; 1982b.
4. Luhmann locates this shift not only on the level of society, but also on the level of the theory of society and social systems. The shift from territorial societies to global society accordingly corresponds to a shift in theory from *identity* to *difference* (*see* Luhmann, 1982b: 133).

5. This formulation is somewhat oversimplified for the sake of presentation. Differentiation is, of course, for all four thinkers mentioned, only one aspect of the shift to modernity. The centrality of the notion of difference in the Luhmannian scheme, however, seems to call for this provisorily simplified formulation if the difference of the Luhmannian model is to be made clear.

6. Luhmann, 1982a: 229 and passim.

7. In addition to running counter to Durkheim and the dominant sociological tradition, conceiving stratification as a form of differentiation is also something not to be found in Luhmann's own earlier work. *See*, e.g., Luhmann, 1970: 148, where one can still read, *"Es gibt nur diese beiden Typen,"* referring to segmentary and functional differentiation as explicitly derived from Durkheim and Parsons.

8. *See* Luhmann, 1984a: 64–65; 1984b: 404–405.

9. *See* Luhmann, 1970: 31–53.

10. Dumont, 1986: 234 and passim. Since Luhmann includes his own theorizing as an object with which his theory must be able to deal, the very central importance of the concept of *selection* in his theory reflects the fact that his theory has as a prime condition of its own possibility the modern society in which it is created (*see* Luhmann, 1984b: 9). This centrality to some extent echoes Berger's analysis (1980) of modern consciousness as being characterized by *choice* rather than *fate*. Although the two analyses are similar, Berger's obsession with *integration* and *consciousness* does not allow him to go beyond the relation of the individual and society to a relatively separate analysis of societal structure as such—based, for instance, as with Luhmann, on *differentiation* and *communication*.

11. *See* Innis, 1972.

12. *See* Luhmann, 1980, vol. 1: 72–161. The important role of self-conceptions in the Luhmannian scheme of things can be seen in that these operate very much like "dominant ideologies." Although coming at the matter from a different angle, the analysis presented here would agree with Abercrombie, Hill, and Turner (1980) to the effect that, based on theoretical and empirical observations, modern society does not have a dominant ideology.

13. *See* Meyer, 1980.

14. Economically based analysis of the world-system is particularly associated with the name of Immanuel Wallerstein (e.g., Wallerstein, 1974) and "Political Economy of the World-System Annuals" (e.g., Bergesen, 1983).

15. *See*, e.g., Wuthnow, 1983: 60–61.

16. E.g., Robertson, 1987; Wuthnow, 1983.

17. Durkheim, 1933: 396 and passim; 1951: 312–20.

18. Parsons, 1968: 461–62, 1971: 4–26.

19. Robertson and Chirico, 1985; Robertson, 1985.

20. Luhmann's own hitherto most thorough presentation of the fundamental theoretical perspectives at issue here is 1984b. My presentation is based on this work, other references serving for specific clarification and application.

21. *See* Robbins and Robertson, 1987.

22. Luhmann is therefore implicitly attempting to overcome the opposition of functional and conflict theories in sociology by showing that there are differences inherent in the very idea of function, differences that can be expressed in conflict. *See* Luhmann's chapter on contradiction and conflict (in 1984b).

23. Parsons, 1971: 27.

24. *See* Luhmann, 1984b: 141 and passim.

25. What is being discussed here is to a large extent the familiar shift from ascription to achievement—Parsons's pattern variable of quality/performance (*see* Parsons, 1951: 63–64).

26. Affirmative action programs and the like, far from being counterindicative of such a negative inclusion, actually confirm it, since they are intended to cancel the effect of past discrimination on an extrafunctional basis so that only functional criteria can operate in the future.

27. Here is where a discussion of Parsons's concept of "adaptive upgrading" would fit in—along with Durkheim's emphasis on an increase in the division of labor under conditions of modernity (*see* Parsons, 1971: 11; Durkheim, 1933).

28. Like Parsons, Luhmann discusses this relation primarily under the heading of interpenetration. Although there are many similarities between the two uses of the term, Luhmann's conception rejects the central Parsonian notion of "zones" of interpenetration principally because they contradict his central idea of systems as consisting of system/environment boundaries based on self-referential selection (*see* Parsons, 1971: 6–7; Luhmann, 1984b: 289 and passim). Far from being merely an esoteric difference in principles of theory construction, this difference in fact reflects the fundamental difference in how modern society is to be understood that is the subject of this chapter. For a critique of Luhmann's position on precisely this basis, see Münch (1980: 20 and passim).

29. E.g., Luhmann, 1982a: 324 and passim, 1984a, 1984b: 360–61.

30. *See* Luhmann, 1984b: 618.

31. For a critique of Luhmann's position on this point from an explicitly theological point of view, *see* Scholz, 1981.

32. *See* Luhmann, 1982a: 69–89.

33. *See* Meyer, 1980.

34. Here is where analyses fit that see current and recurrent crisis in the world-system as necessarily leading to transition or revolution (e.g., Wallerstein, 1983).

35. E.g., Robertson, 1985; Robertson and Chirico, 1985; Simpson, 1987; Wuthnow, 1983.

36. Luhmann, 1982b: 138.

37. Smith, 1981; Küng, 1987; Robertson, 1985. I have elsewhere suggested as much myself (Beyer, 1984: 196–97).

38. *See* Robertson, 1985.

39. The variety makes it meaningful to research the types of groupings and their corresponding solidarities or self-descriptions (*see*, e. g., Lechner, 1987).

40. Wuthnow (1983: 60), in reference to Foucault and Wallerstein in the context of the possibilities for conceiving global social systems.

CHAPTER 5

1. *See* Holleman, 1987.

2. Robertson, 1986.

3. *See* Moore, 1966; Skocpol, 1979.

4. *See*, e.g., Bruce, 1986, 1987; Kimmel and Tavakol, 1986; Kramer, 1987; Meacham, 1987; Mead, 1975; Pankhurst, 1986; Ramet, 1987; Robertson, 1986;

Satha-Anand, 1987; Shams al-Din, 1985; Simpson, 1986; Tamney, 1987; von der Mehden, 1986; Wallis, Bruce, and Taylor, 1986.

5. *See* the essays in Glassman and Swatos, 1986.

6. *See* the work on political sectarianism by O'Toole (1976, 1977).

7. Swatos, 1979.

8. Moore, 1966.

9. While I take up the definition question in the sociology of religion in greater detail in Chapter 9, it should be clear here that I reject the functionalist definition that would make whatever-sociocultural-systems-gravitate-around their "religion." My own approach is "situational" (*see* Swatos, 1984), resting preeminently upon the self-definitions of the participants in the action system.

10. See, 1986.

11. Pétursson, 1988. It is important to note, however, than neither See nor Pétursson sees these language-based cultures as irreligious; rather, their cultural identity symbols have a this-worldly, rather than supernatural, focus. Pétursson (1983) shows very clearly that the Icelandic church in fact served as the agent of language preservation during the Danish colonial period.

12. *See* Shams al-Din, 1985.

13. There are a variety of helpful sources here, some of which pay more attention to the religious variable, some less. *See*, first, the country-by-country accounts in Barrett, 1982; then Adriance, "Paradox"; Eckstein, 1976; Eckstein and Evans, 1978; Kramer, 1987; Meacham, 1987; Novak, 1986; Planas, 1986; Robertson, 1986.

14. Moore, 1966: 490–93.

15. This question is raised in several important respects by Garrett, 1986; Robertson, 1986; and Novak, 1986.

16. *See* the review by Willner and Willner (1965) and the various critiques cited in the essays in Glassman and Swatos (1986).

17. Glassman and Swatos, 1986: 179–203.

18. *See* MacPherson, 1962.

19. *See* Glassman and Swatos, 1986: 73–81.

20. Wuthnow, 1980.

21. Robertson, 1986.

22. This same point is made by Nasr, 1987.

23. Schoenfeld, 1987.

24. Lechner, 1987: 38; *see* Robertson, 1983, 1985, 1987.

25. "We did not want oil, we did not want independence, we wanted Islam." (Ayatollah Khomeini, quoted in Kimmel and Tavakol, 1986: 112.)

26. *See* Swatos, 1988.

27. This section on boundaries is dependent upon Mernissi, 1987.

28. *See* Campbell, 1972.

29. "Conversion" is a complicated process that has meant different things at different times and places. Certainly in modernity it is not an all-or-nothing thing, nor is it restricted to the right or the left. In general, however, Warner (1988) seems correct in saying that on the right there is greater emphasis on "naming the Name," while on the left, priority is given to "doing the deed." These helpful, if facile, turns of phrase must also be supplemented by the realization that the left and the right also each calls in its own way for abstaining

from specific wrong deeds. For the right these will be things like not renting an X-rated video or cursing; for the left, they may be not buying the product of a company doing business in South Africa or making racist remarks. These kinds of things can be fairly easily generalized to the nation-state level in legal codes.

30. *See* Sánchez, 1987.
31. *See* Merle, 1987.
32. *See* Thompson, 1987.
33. *See* Nielsson, 1985; Tiryakian and Nevitte, 1985.
34. Moore, 1966; Nordlinger, 1981; Skocpol, 1979.
35. Swatos, 1984, 1987.

CHAPTER 6

1. Gilbert, 1980: xi.
2. Barrett, 1982: 7.
3. Ibid., 3.
4. Caplow, Bahr, and Chadwick, 1983.
5. Appelbaum, 1970.
6. Bell, 1980: 326–27.
7. Sharot, Ayalon, and Ben-Rafael, 1986: 193.
8. E.g., Berger, 1969: 107–10; Dobbelaere, 1981; Fenn, 1978; Martin, 1978.
9. Chadwick, 1975; Gilbert, 1980.
10. Stark and Bainbridge, 1985.
11. Robertson and Chirico, 1985; Lechner, 1985.
12. Bendix and Berger, 1959.
13. Durkheim, 1915.
14. Malinowski, 1926: 74–80; Douglas, 1982: 18.
15. Durkheim, 1951: 158–62; Bell, 1980.
16. Barrett, 1982: 5.
17. Desert News, 1985.
18. Duke and Johnson, "Exploitation, Oppression."
19. Duke and Johnson, "Atheists and Nonreligious."
20. Berger, 1969: 108.
21. Duke and Johnson, "Atheists and Nonreligious."
22. Barrett, 1982: 136.
23. Duke and Johnson, 1983.
24. Stark and Bainbridge, 1985.
25. A revised and expanded version of a paper published in the *Review of Religious Research* 30 (March, 1989); © Religious Research Association, used by permission.

Chapter 7

1. See Lijphart, 1979; Mayer and Smith, 1985; Michelat and Simon, 1977; Rose, 1974; Rose and Urwin, 1969; but Broughton and Rudd (1984), however, for a good discussion of the need to think critically about the concept of secularization.

2. Inglehart, 1984.
3. Berger, 1982; Percheron, 1982.
4. Wald, 1983; *see* Barnes, 1966, 1974.
5. Benson and Williams, 1982.
6. Mac Iver, 1989.
7. *See* Lijphart, 1975.
8. Madeley, 1982, 1986.
9. Inglehart, 1977.
10. Percheron, 1982.
11. *See* Fox, 1984.
12. Inglehart and Klingemann, 1976; Whyte, 1974.
13. Rochon, 1988.
14. Gilson, 1962.
15. Fogarty, 1957; *see* Irving, 1979; Whyte, 1981.
16. Hostiou, 1968.
17. Hainsworth, 1981.
18. Ibid.; Mac Iver, 1984.
19. Rokeach, 1969.
20. Inglehart, 1977.
21. Ardagh, 1982.
22. Berger, 1982.
23. Mill, 1861.

CHAPTER 8

1. Weber, 1930.
2. *See* Turner, 1985; Fischoff, 1944; Green, 1959.
3. Duke, 1983.
4. Kainz, 1984: 101–102.
5. Ibid., 103.
6. Kristol, 1977.
7. Novak, 1980: 197–98.
8. Poggi, 1983: 7.
9. Eisenstadt, 1978: 200.
10. Cohen, 1985: 289.
11. McCord, 1965.
12. Reisman, Denney, and Glazer, 1953; Mills, 1956.
13. Przeworski, 1986.
14. Gastil, 1980.
15. Barrett, 1982.
16. Ibid.
17. Almond and Coleman, 1960; Lipset, 1960.

CHAPTER 9

1. Hadden, 1987: 588.
2. Robertson, 1971, 1974, 1978, 1982.

3. Shiner, 1967.
4. Hadden, 1987: 598, 609, and passim.
5. Weber, 1978: 399.
6. Bellah, 1967; *see* Mathisen, 1989.
7. Runciman, 1970: 98.
8. Sahay, 1976: 167.
9. Smith, 1984: 28–29.
10. Vidich and Lyman, 1984: 78.
11. As with civil religion, so too with "religious evolution," the Parsonian misadventure is perpetuated by Bellah (1964).
12. Mills, 1959: 32–33.
13. *See*, e.g., Burke, 1978; Heller, 1981; Reay, 1985; Scarisbrick, 1984; Thomas, 1971.
14. Paterson, 1982: 26.
15. Glock, 1988.
16. Durkheim, 1977: 324.
17. Durkheim, 1979: 66.
18. Hall, 1987: 161.
19. Martin, 1969: 22
20. Swatos, 1976: 130.
21. Redekop, 1967: 149.
22. *See* Kivisto, 1986: 174.
23. *See* Berger and Luckmann, 1967.
24. Wallis and Bruce, 1986.
25. Bainbridge, 1987.
26. Homans, 1967.
27. Lewis, 1986: 8.
28. In addition to Berger and Luckmann, 1967, *see* Berger and Luckmann, 1963.
29. Miller, 1975: 157. I agree with Miller that many "individuals are not threatened by living out of more than one stock of knowledge," but also *some are—* this latter aspect he too much minimizes. I also particularly disagree with his rather sanguine functionalist conclusion that everybody is somehow "religious."

Bibliography

Abercrombie, Nicholas, Stephen Hill, and Bryan S. Turner. 1980. *The Dominant Ideology Thesis*. London: Allen & Unwin.

Adriance, Madeleine. Forthcoming. "The Paradox of Institutionalization: The Roman Catholic Church in Chile and Brazil." *Sociological Analysis*.

Alexander, Jeffrey C. 1981–84. *Theoretical Logic in Sociology*. 4 vols. Berkeley: University of California Press.

Almond, Gabriel A., and James S. Coleman, eds. 1960. *The Politics of Developing Areas*. Princeton , N.J.: Princeton University Press.

Appelbaum, Richard P. 1970. *Theories of Social Change*. Chicago: Markham.

Ardagh, John. 1982. *France in the 1980s*. New York: Penguin Books.

Aron, Raymond. 1966. "The Anarchical Order of Power." *Daedalus* 95: 479–502.

Bainbridge, William Sims. 1987. Review of Roy Wallis and Steve Bruce, *Sociological Theory, Religion and Collective Action*. *Sociological Analysis* 48: 177–78.

Barnes, Samuel. 1966. "Ideology and the Organization of Conflict." *Journal of Politics* 3: 513–30.

————. 1974. "Italy: Religion and Class in Electoral Behavior." In *Electoral Behavior: A Comparative Handbook*, edited By Richard Rose, 171–225. New York: Free Press.

Barrett, David B., ed. 1982. *World Christian Encyclopedia*. New York: Oxford University Press.

Beckford, James A., ed. 1986. *New Religious Movements and Rapid Social Change*. London: Sage.

Bell, Daniel. 1962. *The End of Ideology*. New York: Free Press.

————. 1980. "The Return of the Sacred?" In *The Winding Passage*, 324–54. New York: Basic Books.

Bellah, Robert N. 1964. "Religious Evolution." *American Sociological Review* 64: 358–74.

————. 1967. "Civil Religion in America." *Daedalus* 96: 1–21.

Bendix, Reinhard, and Bennett Berger. 1959. "Images of Society and Problems of Concept Formation in Sociology." In *Symposium on Sociological Theory*, edited by Llewellyn Gross, 92–118. Evanston, Ill.: Row, Peterson.

Benson, Peter L., and Dorothy L. Williams. 1982. *Religion on Capital Hill*. New York: Harper & Row.

Berger, Peter L. 1969. *The Sacred Canopy*. Garden City, N.Y.: Doubleday.

———. 1980. *The Heretical Imperative*. Garden City, N.Y.: Doubleday.

Berger, Peter L., and Thomas Luckmann. 1963. "Sociology of Religion and Sociology of Knowledge." *Sociology and Social Research* 47: 417–27.

———. 1967. *The Social Construction of Reality*. Garden City, N.Y.: Doubleday.

Berger, Suzanne. 1982. "Introduction." *West European Politics* 5: 1–7.

Bergesen, Albert. 1980. "From Utilitarianism to Globology." In *Studies of the Modern World-System*, edited by Albert J. Bergesen, 1–12. New York: Academic Press.

———, ed. 1983. *Crises in the World-System*. Beverly Hills, Calif.: Sage.

Beyer, Peter. 1984. "Religion in Modern Society." In *Religion and the Sociology of Knowledge*, edited by Barbara Hargrove, 167–203. Lewistown, N.Y.: Mellen.

Boli-Bennett, John. 1979. "The Ideology of Expanding State Authority in National Constitutions, 1870–1970." In *National Development and the World-System*, edited by John W. Meyer and Michael T. Hannan, 222–37, Chicago: University of Chicago Press.

———. 1980. "Global Integration and the Universal Increase of State Dominance, 1910–1970." In *Studies of the Modern World-System*, edited by Albert Bergesen, 77–107. New York: Academic Press.

Broughton, David, and Christopher Rudd. 1984. "Secularization and Partisan Preferences." *European Journal of Political Research* 12: 445–50.

Bruce, Steve. 1986. "Protestantism and Politics in Scotland and Ulster." In *Prophetic Religions and Politics*, edited by Jeffrey K. Hadden and Anson Shupe, 410–29. New York: Paragon House.

———. 1987. *"God Save Ulster!"* Oxford: Oxford University Press.

Bull, Hedley. 1987. "The Revolt against the West." In *The Expansion of International Society*, edited by Hedley Bull and Adam Watson, 217–28. Oxford: Clarendon Press.

Burke, Peter. 1978. *Popular Culture in Early Modern Europe*. New York: Harper & Row.

Calvin, John. 1960 [1559]. *Institutes of the Christian Religion*. Philadelphia: Westminster Press.

Campbell, Colin. 1972. *Toward a Sociology of Irreligion*. London: Macmillan.

Caplow, Theodore, Howard M. Bahr, and Bruce A. Chadwick. 1983. *All Faithful People*. Minneapolis: University of Minnesota Press.

Cassese, Antonio. 1986. *International Law in a Divided World*. Oxford: Clarendon Press.

Chadwick, Owen. 1975. *The Secularization of the European Mind in the Nineteenth Century*. Cambridge: Cambridge University Press.

Chirot, Daniel, and Thomas D. Hall. 1982. "World-System Theory." *Annual Review of Sociology* 8: 81–106.

Cohen, Ira J. 1985. "The Underemphasis on Democracy in Marx and Weber."

In *A Weber-Marx Dialogue*, edited by Robert J. Antonio and Ronald M. Glassman, 274–99. Lawrence: University Press of Kansas.

Desert News. 1985. *Church Almanac*. Salt Lake City: Desert News.

Dobbelaere, Karel. 1981. *Secularization*. London: Sage.

Douglas, Mary. 1982. "The Effects of Modernization on Religious Change." *Daedalus* 111: 1–19.

Duke, James T. 1983. *Issues in Sociological Theory*. Washington, D.C.: University Press of America.

Duke, James T., and Barry L. Johnson. 1983. "Lo Here and Lo There: Religious Ferment, Modernization, and Denominational Membership in Comparative Perspective." Paper presented at the Conference Internationale de Sociologie des Religions, London.

————. Forthcoming. "Atheists and Nonreligious People: Who, Where, and Why?"

————. Forthcoming. "Exploitation, Oppression and Liberation as Causes of Religious Change." In *Religion, Oppression, Liberation*, edited by Karol Borowski.

Dumont, Louis. 1986. *Essays on Individualism*. Chicago: University of Chicago Press.

Durkheim, Emile. 1915. *The Elementary Forms of the Religious Life*. London: Allen & Unwin.

————. 1933. *The Division of Labor in Society*. New York: Free Press.

————. 1951. *Suicide*. Glencoe, Ill.: Free Press.

————. 1977. *The Evolution of Educational Thought*. London: Routledge & Kegan Paul.

————. 1979. *Durkheim's Essays on Morals and Education*. London: Routledge & Kegan Paul.

Eckstein, Susan. 1976. *The Impact of Revolution: A Comparative Analysis of Mexico and Bolivia*. London: Sage.

Eckstein, Susan, and Peter Evans. 1978. "Revolution as Cataclysm and Coup: Political Transformation and Economic Development in Mexico and Brazil." *Comparative Studies in Sociology* 1: 129–55.

Eisenstadt, S. N., ed. 1968. *The Protestant Ethic and Modernization*. New York: Basic Books.

————. 1978. *Revolution and the Transformation of Societies*. New York: Free Press.

Esposito, John. 1984. *Islam and Politics*. Syracuse, N.Y.: Syracuse University Press.

Fenn, Richard. 1978. *Toward a Theory of Secularization*. Storrs, Conn.: Society for the Scientific Study of Religion.

Fischoff, Ephraim. 1944. "The Protestant Ethic and the Spirit of Capitalism: The History of a Controversy." *Social Research* 11: 61–71.

Fogarty, M. 1957. *Christian Democracy in Western Europe, 1820–1953*. South Bend, Ind.: University of Notre Dame Press.

Fox, John. 1984. *Linear Statistical Models and Related Methods*. New York: Wiley.

Fu, Charles Wei-hsun, and Gerhard E. Spiegler. 1987. *Movements and Issues in World Religions*. Westport, Conn.: Greenwood Press.

Garrett, William R. 1986. "Religion and the Legitimation of Violence." In *Proph-*

etic Religions and Politics, edited by Jeffrey K. Hadden and Anson Shupe, 103–22. New York: Paragon House.

Gastil, Raymond D. 1980. *Freedom in the World: Political and Civil Liberties.* New York: Freedom House.

Gilbert, Alan D. 1980. *The Making of Post-Christian Britain.* London: Longman.

Gilson, Etienne. 1962. "L'unité spirituelle de l'Europe du moyen age à l'heure actuelle." In *L'Unification européenne, réalité et problemes.* Bolzano: Typografia Athesia.

Glassman, Ronald M., and William H. Swatos, Jr., eds. 1986. *Charisma, History, and Social Structure.* Westport, Conn.: Greenwood Press.

Glassman, Ronald M., William H. Swatos, Jr., and Paul L. Rosen, eds. 1987. *Bureaucracy against Democracy and Socialism.* Westport Conn.: Greenwood Press.

Glock, Charles Y. 1988. "The Ways the World Works." *Sociological Analysis* 49: 93–103.

Green, Robert W., ed. 1959. *Protestantism and Capitalism: The Weber Thesis and Its Critics.* Boston: Heath.

Hadden, Jeffrey K. 1987. "Toward Desacralizing Secularization Theory." *Social Forces* 65: 587–611.

Hadden, Jeffrey K., and Anson Shupe, eds. 1986. *Prophetic Religions and Politics.* New York: Paragon House.

Hainsworth, Paul. 1981. "Northern Ireland: A European Role?" *Journal of Common Market Studies* 20: 1–15.

Hall, Robert T. 1987. *Emile Durkheim: Ethics and the Sociology of Morals.* Westport, Conn.: Greenwood Press.

Heller, Agnes. 1981. *Renaissance Man.* New York: Schocken.

Herf, Jeffrey. 1984. *Reactionary Modernism.* Cambridge: Cambridge University Press.

Hofstadter, Douglas R. 1979. *Gödel, Escher, Bach: An Eternal Golden Braid.* New York: Basic Books.

Holleman, Warren Lee. 1987. *The Human Rights Movement.* New York: Praeger.

Homans, George C. 1967. *The Nature of Social Science.* New York: Harcourt, Brace, Jovanovich.

Honigsheim, Paul. 1968. *On Max Weber,* New York: Free Press.

Hostiou, Rene. 1968. *Robert Schuman et l'Europe.* Paris: Editions Cujas.

Inglehart, Ronald. 1977. *The Silent Revolution: Changing Values and Political Styles among Western Publics.* Princeton, N.J.: Princeton University Press.

———. 1984. "The Changing Structures of Political Cleavages in Western Society." In *Electoral Change in Advanced Industrialized Democracies,* edited by Russel J. Dalton, Scott Flanagan, and Paul Allen Beck, 25–69. Princeton, N.J.: Princeton University Press.

Inglehart, Ronald, and Hans-Dieter Klingemann. 1976. "Party Identification, Ideological Preference and the Left-Right Dimension among Western Mass Publics." In *Party Identification and Beyond,* edited by Ian Budge, Ivor Crewe, and Dennis Farlie, 243–73. London: Wiley.

Innis, Harold A. 1972. *Empire and Communication.* Toronto: University of Toronto Press.

Irving, R. E. M. 1979. "Christian Democracy in Postwar Europe: Conservatism

Writ-large or Distinctive Political Phenomenon?" *Western European Politics* 2(1): 53–68.

Janos, Andrew C. 1986. *Politics and Paradigms*. Stanford, Calif.: Stanford University Press.

Kainz, Howard P. 1984. *Democracy East and West*. London: Macmillan.

Kimmel, Michael S., and Rahmat Tavakol. 1986. "Against Satan: Charisma and Tradition in Iran." In *Charisma, History, and Social Structure*, edited by Ronald M. Glassman and William H. Swatos, Jr., 101–12. Westport, Conn.: Greenwood Press.

Kivisto, Peter. 1986. "The Historic Fate of the Charisma of Reason." In *Charisma, History, and Social Structure*, edited by Ronald M. Glassman and William H. Swatos, Jr., 163–77. Westport, Conn.: Greenwood Press.

Kramer, Jane. 1987. "Letter from the Elysian Fields." *The New Yorker* 63 (March 2): 38–75.

Kristol, Irving. 1977. *Two Cheers for Capitalism*. New York: Basic Books.

Küng Hans. 1987. *Theologie im Aufbruch: Eine ökumenische Grundlegung*. Munich: Piper.

Lechner, Frank J. 1984. "Ethnicity and Revitalization in the Modern World System." *Sociological Inquiry* 17: 243–56.

————. 1985. "Modernity and Its Discontents." In *Neofunctionalism*, edited by Jeffrey Alexander, 157–76. Beverly Hills, Calif.: Sage.

————. 1987. "Modernity and Its Procontents." Paper presented to a joint session at the annual meeting of the Association for the Sociology of Religion/American Sociological Association, Chicago.

Lewis, I. M. 1986. *Religion in Context*. Cambridge: Cambridge University Press.

Lijphart, Arend. 1975. *The Politics of Accommodation: Pluralism and Democracy in the Netherlands*. Berkeley: University of California Press.

————. 1979. "Religious versus Linguistic versus Class Voting: The 'Crucial Experiment' of Comparing Belgium, Canada, South Africa and Switzerland." *American Political Science Review* 73: 442–58.

Lipset, Seymour Martin. 1960. "Economic Development and Democracy." In *Political Man*, 27–63. Garden City, N.Y.: Doubleday.

Luckmann, Thomas. 1967. *The Invisible Religion*. London: Macmillan.

Luhmann, Niklas. 1970. *Soziologische Aufklärung 1: Aufsätze zur Theorie sozialer Systeme*. Opladen: Westdeutscher.

————. 1975. *Soziologische Aufklärung 2: Aufsätze zur Theorie der Gesellschaft*. Opladen: Westdeutscher Verlag.

————. 1980. *Gesellschaftsstruktur und Semantik*. 2 vols. Frankfurt: Suhrkamp.

————. 1982a. *The Differentiation of Society*. New York: Columbia University Press.

————. 1982b. "The World Society as a Social System." *International Journal of General Systems* 8: 131–38.

————. 1984a. "The Self-Description of Society." *International Journal of Comparative Sociology* 25: 59–72.

————. 1984b. *Soziale Systeme*. Frankfurt: Suhrkamp.

McCord, William. 1965. *The Springtime of Freedom*. New York: Oxford University Press.

Mac Iver, Martha Abele. 1984. "Militant Protestant Political Ideology: Ian Paisley and the Reformation Tradition." Ph.D. diss., University of Michigan.

_____. 1989. "A Clash of Symbols in Northern Ireland: Differences between Extremist and Moderate Protestant Elites." *Review of Religious Research* 30: 4.

MacPherson, C. B. 1962. *The Political Theory of Possessive Individualism*. Oxford: Oxford University Press.

Madeley, John. 1982. "Politics and the Pulpit: The Case of Protestant Europe." *West European Politics* 5: 149–71.

_____. 1986. "Prophets, Priests and the Polity: European Christian Democracy in a Developmental Perspective." In *Prophetic Religions and Politics*, edited by Jeffrey K. Hadden and Anson Shupe, 365–90. New York: Paragon House.

Malinowski, Bronislaw. 1926. *Crime and Custom in Savage Society*. Totowa, N.J.: Littlefield & Adams.

Marshall, T. H. 1977. *Class, Citizenship, and Social Development*. Chicago: University of Chicago Press.

Martin, David. 1969. *The Religious and the Secular*. New York: Schocken.

_____. 1978. *A General Theory of Secularization*. Oxford: Blackwell.

Mayer, Lawrence, and Roland E. Smith. 1985. "Feminism and Religiosity: Female Electoral Behavior in Western Europe." *West European Politics* 8(4): 38–49.

Mathisen, James A. 1989. "Twenty Years after Bellah: Whatever Happened to American Civil Religion?" *Sociological Analysis* 50: 129–46.

Meacham, Carl E. 1987. "Changing of the Guard: New Relations between Church and State in Chile." *Journal of Church and State* 29: 411–33.

Mead, George H. 1934. *Mind, Self, and Society*. Chicago: University of Chicago Press.

Mead, Sidney E. 1975. *The Nation with the Soul of a Church*. New York: Harper & Row.

Merle, Marcel. 1987. *The Sociology of International Relations*. Leamington Spa, England: Berg.

Mernissi, Fatima. 1987. "Moslem Women and Fundamentalism." In *Beyond the Veil*, vii–xxix. Bloomington: Indiana University Press.

Meyer, John W. 1980. "The World Polity and the Authority of the Nation-State." In *Studies of the Modern World-System*, edited by Albert Bergesen, 109–37. New York: Academic Press.

Meyer, John W., and Michael T. Hannan. 1979. *National Development and the World-System*. Chicago: University of Chicago Press.

Meyer, Marshall W., William Stevenson, and Stephen Webster. 1985. *Limits to Bureaucratic Growth*. New York: De Gruyter.

Michelat, Guy, and Michel Simon. 1977. "Religion, Class, and Politics." *Comparative Politics* 10: 159–86.

Mill, John Stuart. 1861. *Considerations on Representative Government*. London: Parker, Son and Bourne.

Miller, Donald E. 1975. "Religion, Social Change, and the Expansive Life Style." *International Yearbook of Knowledge and Religion* 9: 149–59.

Mills, C. Wright. 1956. *The Power Elite*. New York: Oxford University Press.

_____. 1959. *The Sociological Imagination*. New York: Oxford University Press.

Modelski, George. 1978. "The Long Cycle of Global Politics and the Nation-
State." *Comparative Studies in Society and History* 20: 214–35.
_____. 1983. "Long Cycles of World Leadership." In *Contending Approaches
to World-System Analysis,* edited by William R. Thompson, 115–39. Beverly
Hills, Calif.: Sage.
Moore, Barrington, Jr. 1966. *Social Origins of Dictatorship and Democracy.* Boston:
Beacon.
Münch, Richard. 1980. "Über Parsons zu Weber." *Zeitschrift für Soziologie* 9: 18–
53.
_____. 1982. *Theorie des Handelns.* Frankfurt: Suhrkamp.
Nasr, Sayyed Hossein. 1987. *Traditional Islam in the Modern World.* London: KPI.
Nelson, Benjamin. 1973. "Civilizational Complexes and Intercivilizational En-
counters." *Sociological Analysis* 34: 79–105.
Nettl, J. P., and Roland Robertson. 1968. *International Systems and the Moderni-
zation of Societies.* New York: Basic Books.
Nielsson, Gunnar P. 1985. "States and 'Nation-Groups': A Global Taxonomy."
In *New Nationalisms of the Developed West,* edited by Edward A. Tiryakian
and Ronald Rogowski, 27–56. Boston: Allen & Unwin.
Nordlinger, Eric A. 1981. *On the Autonomy of the Democratic State.* Cambridge,
Mass.: Harvard University Press.
Novak, Michael, ed. 1980. *Democracy and Mediating Structures.* Washington, D.C.:
American Enterprise Institute.
_____. 1986. *Will It Liberate?* New York: Paulist Press.
O'Toole, Roger. 1976. " 'Underground' Traditions in the Study of Sectarianism."
Journal for the Scientific Study of Religion 15: 145–56.
_____. 1977. *The Precipitous Path.* Toronto: Martin.
Pankhurst, Jerry G. 1986. "Comparative Perspectives on Religion and Regime
in Eastern Europe and the Soviet Union." In *Prophetic Religions and Politics,*
edited by Jeffrey K. Hadden and Anson Shupe, 272–306. New York:
Paragon House.
Parsons, Talcott. 1937. *The Structure of Social Action.* Glencoe, Ill.: Free Press.
_____. 1951 *The Social System.* New York: Free Press.
_____. 1968. "Systems Analysis: Social Systems." *Encyclopedia of the Social
Sciences* 15: 458–73.
_____. 1971. *The System of Modern Societies.* Englewood Cliffs, N.J.: Prentice-
Hall.
Paterson, John. 1982. Kildare: The Cathedral Church of Saint Brioid. Kildare:
No pulbisher given.
Percheron, Annick. 1982. "Religious Acculturation and Political Socialisation in
France." *West European Politics* 5: 8–31.
Pétursson, Pétur. 1983. *Church and Social Change.* Helsingborg, Sweden: Plus
Ultra.
_____. 1988. "The Relevance of Secularization in Iceland." *Social Compass* 35:
107–24.
Planas, Ricardo. 1986. *Liberation Theology.* Kansas City, Mo.: Sheed & Ward.
Poggi, Gianfranco. 1983. *Calvinism and the Capitalist Spirit.* Amherst: University
of Massachusetts Press.
Przeworski, Adam. 1986. "Some Problems in the Study of the Transition to

Democracy." In *Transitions from Authoritarian Rule*, edited by Guillermo
  O'Donnell, Philippe C. Schmitter, and Laurence Whitehead, 47–63. Bal-
  timore, Md.: Johns Hopkins University Press.
Ramet, Pedro. 1987. *Cross and Commissar*. Bloomington: Indiana University Press.
Reay, Barry, ed. 1985. *Popular Culture in Seventeenth-Century England*. New York:
  St. Martin's Press.
Redekop, Calvin. 1967. "Toward an Understanding of Religion and Social Sol-
  idarity." *Sociological Analysis* 27: 149–61.
Riesman, David, Reuel Denney, and Nathan Glazer. 1953. *The Lonely Crowd*.
  New Haven: Yale University Press.
Robbins, Thomas, and Roland Robertson, eds. 1987. *Church-State Relations*. New
  Brunswick, N.J.: Transaction.
Robertson, Roland. 1971. "Sociologists and Secularization." *Sociology* 5: 297–312.
————. 1974. "Religious and Sociological Factors in the Analysis of Secularization." In *Changing Perspectives in the Scientific Study of Religion*, edited
  by Allan W. Eister, 41–60. New York: Wiley.
————. 1978. "Biases in the Analysis of Secularization." In *Meaning and Change*,
  258–76. New York: New York University Press.
————. 1982. "Societies, Individuals and Sociology: Intracivilizational
  Themes." *Theory, Culture & Society* 1: 6–17.
————. 1983. "Religion, Global Complexity and the Human Condition." In
  Absolute Values and the Creation of the New World, 185–212. New York:
  International Cultural Foundation.
————. 1985. "The Sacred and the World-System." In *The Scared in a Secular
  Age*, edited by Phillip E. Hammond, 347–58. Berkeley: University of Cal-
  ifornia Press.
————. 1986. "Liberation Theology in Latin America." In *Prophetic Religions
  and Politics*, edited by Jeffrey K. Hadden and Anson Shupe, 73–102. New
  York: Paragon House.
————. 1987. "Church-State Relations and the World-System." In *Church-State
  Relations*, edited by Thomas Robbins and Roland Robertson, 39–51. New
  Brunswick, N.J.: Transaction.
Robertson, Roland, and JoAnn Chirico. 1985. "Humanity, Globalization, and
  Worldwide Religious Resurgence: A Theoretical Exploration." *Sociological
  Analysis* 46: 219–42.
Robertson, Roland, and Frank Lechner. 1985. "Modernization, Globalization and
  the Problem of Culture in World-Systems Theory." *Theory, Culture &
  Society* 2: 103–17.
Rochon, Thomas R. 1988. *Mobilizing for Peace*. Princeton, N.J.: Princeton Uni-
  versity Press.
Rokeach, Milton. 1969. "Religious Values and Social Compassion." *Review of
  Religious Research* 11:24–39.
Rose, Richard, ed. 1974. *Electoral Behavior: A Comparative Handbook*. New York:
  Free Press.
Rose, Richard, and Dereck Urwin. 1969. "Social Cohesion, Political Parties and
  Strains in Regimes." *Comparative Political Studies* 2: 7–67.
Runciman, W. G. 1970. *Sociology in Its Place*. Cambridge: Cambridge University
  Press.

Sahay, Arun. 1976. "The Concepts of Morality and Religion: A Critique of the Durkheimian World-View." *Sociological Analysis and Theory* 6: 167–85.

Sánchez, José M. 1987. *The Spanish Civil War as a Religious Tragedy*. South Bend, Ind: University of Notre Dame Press.

Satha-Anand, Chaiwat. 1987. *Islam and Violence: A Case Study of Violent Events in the Four Southern Provinces, Thailand, 1976–1981*. Tampa, Fla: USF Monographs in Religion and Public Policy.

Scarisbrick, J. J. 1984. *The Reformation and the English People*. Oxford: Blackwell.

Scholz, Frithard. 1981. *Freiheit als Indifferenz: Alteuropäische Probleme mit der Systemtheorie Niklas Luhmanns*. Frankfurt: Suhrkamp.

Schoenfeld, Eugen. 1987. "Militant Religion." In *Religious Sociology*, edited by William H. Swatos, Jr., 125–37. Westport, Conn.: Greenwood Press.

See, Katherine O'Sullivan. 1986. *First World Nationalisms*. Chicago: University of Chicago Press.

Shams al-Din, Muhammed Mehdi. 1985. *The Rising of Al Husayn*. London: Muhammadi Trust.

Sharot, Stephen, Hannah Ayalon, and Eliezer Ben-Rafael. 1986. "Secularization and the Diminishing Decline of Religion." *Review of Religious Research* 27: 192–207.

Shiner, Larry. 1967. "The Concept of Secularization in Empirical Research." *Journal for the Scientific Study of Religion* 6: 207–20.

Simpson, John H. 1986. "Some Elementary Forms of Authority and Fundamentalist Politics." In *Prophetic Religions and Politics*, edited by Jeffrey K. Hadden and Anson Shupe, 391–409. New York: Paragon House.

————. 1987. "Globalization, the New Religious Right, and the Politics of the Body." *Psychohistory Review* 15(2): 59–75.

Skocpol, Theda. 1979. *States and Social Revolutions*. Cambridge: Cambridge University Press.

Smith, Anthony D. 1981. *The Ethnic Revival*. Cambridge: Cambridge University Press.

————. 1983. "Ethnic Identity and World Order." *Millennium: Journal of International Studies* 12: 147–61.

Smith, Wilfred Cantwell. 1981. *Towards a World Theology*. Philadelphia: Westminster Press.

————. 1984. "On Mistranslated Book Titles." *Religious Studies* 20: 27–42.

Stark, Rodney, and William Sims Bainbridge. 1985. *The Future of Religion*. Berkeley and Los Angeles: University of California Press.

Swanson, Guy E. 1967. *Religion and Regime*. Ann Arbor: University of Michigan Press.

Swatos, William H., Jr. 1976. "Weber or Troeltsch? Methodology, Syndrome, and the Development of Church-Sect Theory." *Journal for the Scientific Study of Religion* 15: 129–44.

————. 1979. *Into Denominationalism: The Anglican Metamorphosis*. Storrs, Conn.: Society for the Scientific Study of Religion.

————. 1984. "Religion, Secularization, and Social Process." *New England Sociologist* 5: 95–112.

————, ed. 1987. *Religious Sociology*. Westport, Conn.: Greenwood Press.

————. 1988. "Picketing Satan Enfleshed at 7-Eleven." *Review of Religious Research* 30: 73–82.

Tamney, Joseph B. 1987. "Islam's Popularity: The Case of Indonesia." *Southeast Asian Journal of Social Science* 15: 53–65.

Thomas, Keith. 1971. *Religion and the Decline of Magic*. London: Weidenfeld & Nicolson.

Thompson, Ann. 1987. *Barbary and Enlightenment*. Leiden: Brill.

Tilly, Charles. 1985. *Big Structures, Large Processes, Huge Comparisons*. New York: Russell Sage.

Tiryakian, Edward A., and Neil Nevitte. 1985. "Nationalism and Modernity." In *New Nationalisms of the Developed West*, edited by Edward A. Tiryakian and Ronald Rogowski, 57–86. Boston: Allen & Unwin.

Turner, Stephen P. 1985. "Explaining Capitalism." In *A Weber-Marx Dialogue*, edited by Robert J. Antonio and Ronald M. Glassman, 167–88. Lawrence: University Press of Kansas.

Vidich, Arthur J., and Stanford M. Lyman. 1984. *American Sociology*. New Haven, Conn.: Yale University Press.

Voll, John Obert. 1982. *Islam: Continuity and Change in the Modern World*. Boulder, Colo.: Westview Press.

von der Mehden, Fred R. 1986. *Religion and Modernization in Southeast Asia*. Syracuse, N.Y.: Syracuse University Press.

Wald, Kenneth. 1983. *Crosses on the Ballot*. Princeton, N.J.: Princeton University Press.

Wallerstein, Immanuel. 1974. *The Modern World-System*. New York: Academic Press.

————. 1982. "Crisis as Transition." In *Dynamics of Global Crisis*, edited by Samir Amin et al., 11–54. New York: Monthly Review Press.

————. 1983. "Crisis: The World-Economy, the Movements, and the Ideologies." In *Crises in the World System*, edited by Albert Bergesen, 21–36. Beverly Hills, Calif.: Sage.

Wallis, Roy, and Steve Bruce. 1986. *Sociological Theory, Religion and Collective Action*. Belfast: Queen's University.

Wallis, Roy, Steve Bruce, and David Taylor. 1986. *"No Surrender!": Paisleyism and the Politics of Ethnic Identity in Northern Ireland*. Belfast: Queen's University.

Warner, R. Stephen. 1988. *New Wine in Old Wineskins*. Berkeley: University of California Press.

Weber, Max. 1930. *The Protestant Ethic and the Spirit of Capitalism*. New York: Scribners.

————. 1946. "Politics as a Vocation." In *From Max Weber*, edited by H. H. Gerth and C. Wright Mills, 77–128. New York: Oxford University Press.

————. 1978. *Economy and Society*. Berkeley: University of California Press.

Whyte, John. 1974. "Ireland: Politics without Social Bases." In *Electoral Behavior: A Comparative Handbook*, edited by Richard Rose. New York: Free Press.

————. 1981. *Catholics in Western Democracies*. Dublin: Gill and MacMillan.

Willner, Ann Ruth, and Dorothy Willner. 1965. "The Rise and Role of Charismatic Leaders." *Annals of the American Academy of Political and Social Science* 358: 77–89.

Wilson, Bryan. 1976. *Contemporary Transformations of Religion.* New York: Oxford University Press.

Wilson, John. 1978. *Religion in American Society.* Englewood Cliffs, N.J.: Prentice-Hall.

Wuthnow, Robert. 1978. "Religious Movements and the Transition in World Order." In *Understanding the New Religions,* edited by Jacob Needleman and George Baker, 63–79. New York: Seabury Press.

————. 1980. "World Order and Religious Movements." In *Studies of the Modern World-System,* edited by Albert Bergesen, 57–75. New York: Academic Press.

————. 1983. "Cultural Crises." In *Crises in the World-System,* edited by Albert Bergesen, 57–71. Beverly Hills, Calif.: Sage.

————. 1987. *Meaning and Moral Order.* Berkeley: University of California Press.

Zolberg, Aristide R. 1981. "Origins of the Modern World-System: A Missing Link." *World Politics* 33: 253–81.

————. 1983. "World and System: A Misalliance." In *Contending Approaches in World-System Analysis,* edited by William R. Thompson, 269–90. Beverly Hills, Calif.: Sage.

Index

About the Editor and Contributors

PETER F. BEYER is Assistant Professor in the Department of Religious Studies at the University of Toronto. He has published a translation, with substantial introduction, of Niklas Luhmann's *Religious Dogmatics and the Evolution of Societies*. His current research interests center on the relation of religion to political action in the global context.

JAMES T. DUKE is Professor of Sociology and Chairman of the Department of Sociology at Brigham Young University. He is the author of *Conflict and Power in Social Life* and *Issues in Sociological Theory*, and is now writing an introductory sociology text, *Insights in Social Behavior*. His current research deals with rates of religious change throughout the world, and the interaction of religion with economic, political, and social factors in these nations.

BARRY L. JOHNSON is an Associate Professor of Sociology at Brigham Young University, teaching in both the Department of Sociology and the School of Social Work. In addition to his research interests in the sociology of religion, he and another colleague are conducting a number of studies on incest perpetrators. As part of this work, they are co-editing a book entitled *The Incest Perpetrator: The Family Member No One Wants to Treat*.

FRANK J. LECHNER is Assistant Professor in the Department of Sociology at Emory University. His main research interests and professional publications focus on problems in sociological theory, world-system analysis, the comparative study of religion, and the study of various sociocultural movements, especially those of fundamentalist character.

MARTHA ABELE MAC IVER is Assistant Professor of Political Science at Occidental College. She has conducted research on Protestant fundamentalism and ecumenical reconciliation communities in Northern Ireland and is currently working on a book about the Christian left in the United States.

JOHN H. SIMPSON is Professor of Sociology and Chair, Department of Sociology, University of Toronto. His recent publications include articles on politics and religion and on structural shifts in American society. His current research in the area of globalization focuses on the comparative analysis of globalization theories, but he is also co-author of a number of articles on gender, family, and delinquency.

WILLIAM H. SWATOS, JR. is editor of *Sociological Analysis: A Journal in the Sociology of Religion*, the official journal of the Association for the Sociology of Religion, and a member of the Board of Directors of the Religious Research Association. He is the author of numerous scholarly articles and monographs. His most recent books include *Max Weber: A Bio-Bibliography* (with Peter Kivisto, Greenwood Press, 1988) and *Religious Sociology: Interfaces and Boundaries* (Greenwood Press, 1987). He is currently working on a collection in the comparative history of religion, *Time, Place, and Circumstance: Neo-Weberian Studies in Comparative Religious History*. Professor Swatos teaches a variety of undergraduate courses in sociology and philosophy.

DATE DUE

JAN 3 0 1999			
DEC 2 7 1999			

HIGHSMITH   # 45220